MAYMYO
DAYS

First published in Thailand 2023
by River Books Press, Co., Ltd
396/1 Maharaj Road,
Phraborommaharajawang,
Bangkok 10200 Thailand
Telephone: (66) 2 225-9574, 2 225-0139
Email: order@riverbooksbk.com
www.riverbooksbk.com

Copyright collective work
© River Books 2023

Copyright texts
© Stephen Simmons

Copyright photographs
© Stephen Simmons 2023
except where indicated otherwise

All rights reserved. No part of
this book may be reproduced or
transmitted in any form or by any
means electrical or mechanical
including photocopying, recording
or by any information storage or
retrieval system without the
written permission of the publisher

Editor: Narisa Chakrabongse
Production: Suparat Sudcharoen
Design: Peter Cope

ISBN 978 616 451 076 0

Printed and bound in Thailand
by Sirivatana Interprint Public Co., Ltd

MAYMYO DAYS

STEPHEN SIMMONS

RIVER BOOKS

Shan Traders in Bazaar, Maymyo

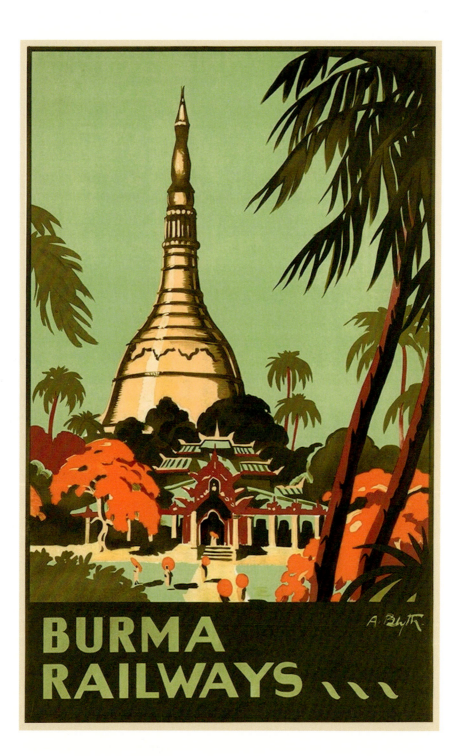

Contents

Foreword 11

Prologue 13

Introduction 15

Maymyo & the Shan Hills 21

The Forest Men 39

The Writer 59

The Mapmaker 73

The Gardener 85

The Soldier 107

The Princesses 119

The Artist 139

The Photographer 167

The Stayers On 187

BURMA

Natural Scale 1:12,000,000 Miles

0 — 50 — 100 — 200

Railways thus

Foreword

By Htein Lin Aung, the Limbin Prince

My grandfather was Prince (Hteik Tin) Maung Kin Kin Gyi, Prince of Limbin (the Limbin Mintha), Prince of Kenaung. He was the son of Konbaung, the brother of King Mindon who was the last but one of the Burmese Kings to rule in Northern Burma. The last King, King Thibaw was sent into exile by the British in 1886 after the 3rd Anglo-Burmese War. My family comes from the Shan hills, that great area to the east of Mandalay which stretches as far as China to the north east, Laos to the east and Thailand to the south. We Shan lived as a number of small states and we did so in complete harmony with one another and with many other Burmese peoples in the hills like the Karen, the Kachins, the Lisu, the Palaung and even, once their rebellions ended, with the Panthay. We were and we are, peace-loving and want nothing more than to be left alone to rule ourselves and to live our lives as we wish.

As soon as the British occupied the area around Maymyo they saw that it was cool, lush and beautiful and they began to settle there and soon the Government would come up to the hills during the hot season to get away from the heat of Rangoon and many British came to live there. My grandmother, Princess Ma Lat married Herbert Bellamy, an Australian in 1928 and they lived in Rangoon. My mother, Princess Yadana Nat Mai was born in 1932. They escaped to India during the Japanese war but when they returned they chose not to live in Rangoon but to go home to Maymyo in the Shan hills.

Like the author, I too have wondered why so many people of talent and of great ability went to live in and around Maymyo. The author cannot put his finger on exactly why they did – he thinks there was 'something in the Shan hills air' and I agree with him. There was a magic to Maymyo, a special ingredient which acted like a drug because it pulled you in and made it difficult ever to leave. But it was a good drug! My father, Mario Postiglione was a very gifted man who was, at the time one of the world's leading authorities on that terrible disease malaria. He married my mother Princess Yadana Nat Mai in 1954 and although at first they went to live in Lashio they soon left and set up home in Maymyo. He was one of many capable, yes, I believe extraordinary people who made this town their home – Maymyo drew them in and kept them there because they loved it (my parents certainly did).

The author has written of artists, soldiers, writers, forest men, gardeners and Princesses for whom Maymyo seemed to have been both their inspiration and their home. I now live in Florence and cannot go back to the Shan hills but the hills and Maymyo itself remain an inspiration and, in my heart, my home and when I read the first draft of this book I felt as if the author, an Englishman, had begun to understand the draw of the hills almost as well as me, a Shan who was born there and who is of the blood.

THE FIRST ENGLISH LADY IN A SHAN BAZAAR

Prologue

MAYMYO, THE HILL STATION OF MANDALAY

Three thousand five hundred feet above the city of Mandalay, the capital of Upper Burma, is the pleasant little hill-station of Maymyo, nestling among the Shan hills. Not long ago an unpretentious village, it is now an important military post, with a garrison of European and native troops, to which have also been added a detachment of Punjabi police. The trade of the place has increased since the British occupation, and the Bazaar, held every five days, is a scene of busy commercial activity. To Maymyo come the traders of distant Shan states, bringing their rice and pickled tea; Panthays from the further confines of Burmah and the almond-eyed merchant from far Cathay, while Shan caravans, with their interminable trains of neatly laden pack-bullocks, pass through weekly on their way to Mandalay.

On bazaar day, Maymyo is seen at its best. Everyone is in holiday attire, and the market place is thronged with a heterogeneous crowd, in colours of gorgeous hues, and with head-dresses of quaint and curious design. Of the latter, a large, flexible betasselled straw hat, convertible by the aid of string into a 'Dolly Varden,' is much affected by male dandies by way of a finishing touch to their silk fur-lined jackets, and silver-mounted 'dahs' or dirks, which are frequently of costly and excellent workmanship. The headgear of the women is somewhat less pretentious. Use, rather than ornament, appears to be consulted; and their sugar-loafed hats of bark, of varied pattern, and consisting almost entirely of brim, amply fulfil this requirement.

As a hill-station and sanatorium, Maymyo may be said to be in its infancy; in fact, its future as such is as yet undecided. It has a possible rival in Koni, a green and salubrious spot, where pine-trees flourish away to the south. But the hard-worked and perspiring toilers of the Golden City are not loth to ride the forty miles and to climb the steep ascent which lie between them and Maymyo, whenever an opportunity is offered.

Even two European ladies have ventured so far, and have braved the discomforts of a long and tedious journey, for the sake of a change to a cool climate, and to feast the eye on vegetation other than tropical. For up here the scenery is more English than Burman. The first arrival of that rarist apparition in the Shan country, an English lady, created the keenest interest and excitement in the breasts of the natives. She was followed everywhere by a gaping and astonished crowd; and on a market day they all jostled one another to obtain a good view of this remarkable figure; while on horseback she filled them still further with awe and wonderment.

In this wild region the lover of orchids will find plenty to occupy and amuse him. Within easy distance of the Fort, are numerous, procurable specimens of those interesting plants, some quaint and uncommon, others merely of local interest, rich in blossoms, but of no great rarity or value. For a few annas a coolie will journey to the hills and distant gorges amidst the mountains, and bring back enough plants to adorn a bungalow; and for a few rupees sufficient to stock a conservatory.

It is to be hoped that this station, possessing such a good climate and other advantages will become to Mandalay what Ootacamund and Darjeeling are to Madras and Calcutta.

Lieutenant A.E. Congdon, 2nd Battalion Royal Munster Fusiliers
Illustrated London News. 8 December 1888

*'Austere, sporting and contemplative;
Maymyo was very clean, hard-working,
hard-playing, exaggeratedly national and
slightly dull. But if unadventurous and simple
by French colonial standards, life in Maymyo
was full of solid comfort.'*

Norman Lewis, Travel Writer

Introduction

OUTSKIRTS OF MAYMYO IN THE SHAN HILLS
Illustrated London News. 8 December 1888

INTRODUCTION

The British occupied Burma for nearly 125 years from 1824 until 1948. The reason was not about trade, which of course is what the flag usually followed. British trade in early 19th century Burma was at best minimal. Nor were they there as the result of pre-planned and premeditated territorial and economic aggression by the British State; no such plans existed, not for Burma anyway. And Burma was not colonised by the British because of 'a fit of absence of mind', as the Victorian historian J.R. Seeley considered was the usual reason for colonisation. Britain's annexation of Burma was the result of two expanding and ultimately colliding empires; King Bagyidaw's westward-looking empire in Burma and the Honourable East India Company's (EIC) eastward-looking empire in India.

In 1767, 40,000 troops of the Ava seated Burmese Konbaung dynasty sacked the Siamese city of Ayutthaya, then the capital of the Ayutthaya Kingdom, which had stretched back, if indirectly, for over 450 years. In doing so, the action destroyed the Ban Phlu Luang dynasty which had ruled for eighty years. The fighting was savage and brutal with many Siamese taken back to Burma as hostages and slaves. The sacking of the capital and consequent loss of life, prestige and wealth scarred Siamese psychology to such an extent that even now the event is raised in everyday conversation as if it had only recently taken place. Despite living largely off the land, the Burmese armies so far from home, became over extended. Shortly after sacking Ayutthaya, Burma itself came under opportunistic attack from China in the north-east, then from a quickly resurgent Siam under General, later King, Taksin, forcing the Burmese to withdraw behind their own borders which they sought rapidly to shore up. In 1784, still hungry for conquest, but cognisant and cautious of well-organised resistance to the east in Siam, the now Amarapura seated King Bodawpaya looked instead to the west, marching into the state of Arakan. Arakanese rebels fled over the border into British-controlled Chittagong from where they mounted sporadic raids back over the border against Burmese forces occupying the Arakan. This unstable situation rumbled on until 1824 when the Burmese, now ruled by the aggressive King Bagyidaw, invaded Manipur and Assam. Pushing on further west they briefly occupied Jainta and Cachar, bringing Burmese forces close to Calcutta – uncomfortably close for the British. The EIC reacted by supporting anti-Burmese rebels in Jainta and Cachar. Discomfort in Calcutta had begun to turn to alarm and the Governor General of Bengal, Lord William Amherst, was forced to act in order to secure his eastern borders and on 5 March 1824 he declared war on the Kingdom of Ava. In the early stages things did not go well for the British, as EIC troops were roundly beaten in early clashes. The Burmese, under the trusted and competent General Bandula, pushed into Bengal, overwhelming the EIC's small army at the Battle of Ramu, just ten miles east of Cox's Bazar. This, in spite of the fact that the EIC army of fewer than 1,000 men was drawn mainly from the 20th and 23rd Regiments of Bengal Native Infantry, a small but well-armed force.

Thereafter, superior weaponry and modern military tactics prevailed and the Burmese were driven out of Assam, Cachar and Manipur concurrent with the despatch by Lord Amherst of 10,000 troops under Sir Archibald Campbell to attack Rangoon. However, the occupation of the city turned out to be quite a simple mission, as the Burmese had withdrawn both troops and populace, giving themselves time to muster a sizeable army under the command of Bandula, well away from Rangoon and from occupying British troops. Once his army had assembled, Bandula unwisely planned a direct frontal attack on the superior weaponry of EIC's British and Indian troops, who had dug in around the Shwedagon Pagoda. The attack was firmly repulsed with the heavy loss of Burmese life. The Burmese army was forced to withdraw up river and Bandula was later killed whilst defending the village of Danabyu in the Irrawaddy Delta.

An anecdote of no significance to our story of Maymyo, yet a point of interest to those drawn to the history of Sarawak, relates to a young officer of the 6th Bengal Native Infantry seriously wounded in this war during a skirmish at Rungpore; he survived – but only just. His name was Lieutenant James

INTRODUCTION

King Thibaw (right), Queen Supayalat (centre) and her sister Princess Supayalay (left)

Brooke. He was shot through the lung and initially left for dead. Had he, because of the severity of his wounds, gone the way of most of the wounded, Sarawak would have had no White Rajah and its history would have been somewhat different. But back to Burma.

After a further defeat at the Battle of Prome in December 1825, the King surrendered and the war formally ended with the signing of the Treaty of Yandabo in February 1826. The treaty ceded the Arakan and Tenasserim to the British – a substantial territorial loss to the Burmese over and above a colossal indemnity of £1m which crippled the Burmese exchequer for years. A tense stand-off was to follow, during which time the British established commercial operations in the country, resulting in clashes with Burmese interests. It was one such confrontation which led to the Second Anglo-Burmese War of 1852-1853, triggered by the Governor of Rangoon, who fined Captains of several British Merchant Navy vessels for allegedly evading certain customs duties. The Captains declared their innocence and the British were outraged. Lord Dalhousie, the Governor General of India, then demanded the cancellation of the fines, a demand to which the Burmese soon acceded. However, the British Naval Squadron in the area under the command of the often-hasty Commodore George Lambert blockaded the Gulf of Martaban and then seized Rangoon at his own discretion, to the fury of Dalhousie. In Ava, King Mindon overthrew his half-brother Pagan and then sued for peace. The British simply ignored him, then seized and occupied Lower Burma. Again, an uneasy 'truce' prevailed for several more decades as the British developed their trade links and strengthened their commercial attachments in this now semi-occupied state, but the precarious nature of the situation was destined not to last.

King Mindon proved to be a popular monarch, as we shall see later, interested in the welfare of his people rather than in territorial gains so desired by many of his predecessors. However, in 1878 when Thibaw succeeded his father to the throne, a rather different state of affairs began to evolve. Thibaw was cruel, unpopular and lacked the charisma of his father and was very much under the control of his manipulative wife Supayalat. Less than a year after succeeding to the throne and consumed with fear of treachery, he tried to ensure his own survival by killing fifty members of his own family, chiefly his own brothers and half-brothers who he believed might well challenge his sovereignty.

Furthermore, Thibaw harboured militarily unrealistic plans to remove the British from Lower Burma, thereby restoring his sovereignty across the whole of the country. To this end he opened a dialogue with England's 'traditional enemy' – the French, who at this point were firmly ensconced in their own Indochinese empire of Vietnam, Cambodia and Laos, yet were looking to expand their influence even further west. The French had offered to build a railway from Lower Burma to Mandalay and establish and capitalise a bank, in

Rajah James Brooke of Sarawak

exchange for trading concessions, which worried the British. Then to compound matters, Thibaw signed an arms deal with the French. For the British, keen to contain the French within their Indochinese territories and to preserve what they saw as their rights to the control of Burmese trade, this was all too much. Matters were complicated further by the spendthrift Thibaw's demand of a loan of Rs (rupees) 22 *lakhs* (a *lakh*, an Indian unit of measure equates to 100,000) from the Bombay Burmah Trading Corporation (BBTC); this coupled with the threat of a fine of Rs 28 *lakhs* on a trumped-up charge of the company failing to pay its timber revenue share to his administration. The company refused the loan and denied the allegation regarding the revenue share. Once again, the British were outraged. Troubled by threats posed by the French link, the British demanded that King Thibaw cede sovereignty for foreign affairs to the British colonial government in Calcutta. When Thibaw refused, the British attacked; there was a brief and bloody skirmish followed by occupation. The taking of Mandalay was not, in the overall scheme of Britain's foreign adventures a costly war, but it was no 'picnic' as Thibaw's troops resisted.

In his *'Sea to Sea: Letters of Travel 1899'*, written after staying at the Pegu Club in Rangoon in March 1889, Rudyard Kipling describes the scene: *'…and I went out into the steamy night, my head ringing with stories of battle, murder and sudden death. I had reached the fringes of the veil which hides Upper Burma and I would have given much to have gone up the river and seen a score of old friends, now jungle-worn men of war. There must be a few hundred men who are fairly behind the scenes of the Burma war – one of the least known and appreciated of our little affairs. The Pegu Club seemed to be full of men on their way up or down and the conversation was but an echo of conquest far away to the north'. And; 'Another voice in the middle of the conversation "they never got that story into the papers but I can tell you we weren't quite as quick in rushing the fort as they made believe. You see Boh Gwee had us in a regular trap and by the time we had closed the line our men were being peppered front and rear: that jungle fighting is the deuce and all"'.*

There had been one set-piece battle – the Battle of Minhla near Mandalay, after which Thibaw surrendered to the British commander, General Sir Harry Prendergast. Three days later Thibaw abdicated and was promptly exiled to India. The kingdom was annexed and Burma became a British colony on 1 January 1886, followed by a province of India the following year, complete with a Lieutenant Governor. Needless to say, annexation was both entirely unwelcome and fiercely resisted. To become a mere province of India infuriated many Burmese, even though this situation was belatedly changed in 1937 as a result of the Act of Separation from India. The Act meant that Burma was no longer administered by Calcutta, but by the Burma Office in London. The designation 'province of India', rankles to this day, almost as much as the annexation itself. The British remained in Burma until Independence was granted on 4 January 1948.

The Battle of Minhla 17 November 1885

'The Pegu Club seemed to be full of men on their way up or down and the conversation was but an echo of conquest far away to the north.'

Rudyard Kipling

Maymyo & the Shan Hills

In his book *'Lords of the Sunset'*, Maurice Collis recalls that the British Empire was *'like an old country house that had been lived in by the same family for generations and that each new generation had added in some way, to the house by acquiring more 'possessions' and that for no particularly good reason, absentmindedness perhaps, some of the best and most beautiful acquisitions wound up not in the drawing room for all to see but in the attic, tucked away and forgotten'*. The Shan States were, thought Collis, stuck in the imperial attic.

The Shan came from the north-west corner of China where there are peoples of the Tibeto-Burman branch of the Mongolian race. The most dominant of these peoples were the Shans or T'ai who over 1,000 years ago had their own Kingdom in Yunnan called Nanchao. Sometime around the middle of the 13th century the Shan were overwhelmed by the Tartars and driven south to the vast area now known as Burma, Thailand, Laos and Cambodia. Dominant at first in what is now Burma, they eventually yielded to the might of the Burmans and retreated to the 60,000 square miles of the (now) Shan hills, each tribe or sub-tribe overlorded by a chieftain or *sawbwa*. The British assumed control over the States after the 3rd Anglo-Burmese War and the subsequent annexation of Upper Burma. The war had been short and as we have seen, not overly bloody (for its time), but of huge importance for Burma. The annexation of Upper Burma was the final act in a long process of antagonism and creeping colonisation which concluded with the inclusion of Burma into the British Empire.

By the time the British arrived in 1886 the Shan hills had long become an easy-to-dominate agglomeration of largely ethnically homogeneous, but tribally diverse statelets whose population amounted to around two million people; this, excluding the Karens, both Black and Red – the colours referring to the clothes which these separate 'sub-branches' wore – and also a smaller number of Kachin and Panthay. The British dealt harshly with resistance post-annexation. While there was a clear difference between the aims of those engaged in annexation resistance and those engaged in 'dacoity' – robbery and lawlessness, the British did not distinguish between the two, an error serving only to further resistance and instability. Instability was compounded by the disbandment of the *Hlutdaw* or King's Advisory Council, along with Thibaw's remnant army and police force. After a while, chastened perhaps by the strength of dissent, but coupled with a degree of political and cultural empathy, they chose not to enter the states all guns blazing, but to approach in a more empathetic and pragmatic fashion. They did so partly on the advice of Chief Commissioner D.M. Smeaton, coupled with recommendations made after an extensive survey of the states by the Commandant of the 3rd Gurkha Rifles, Colonel (later General) Edward Stedman and two civilian officers – A.H. Hildebrand who went on to become Superintendent of the Shan States and J.G. Scott, journalist and later colonial administrator. As a result, the British did not divide up the states into districts, each under the control of a British Deputy Commissioner as was the 'norm', but placed each of the states under the control of its own *sawbwa* along with a British advisor. In time these advisors came to constitute what eventually evolved into the Burma Frontier Service. A council of chiefs was convened with a member of the Frontier Service as Chairman. The council proved to be a success, enabling hitherto warring states to negotiate and work together for the common good of all of the Shan States.

A book about an old British hill station could easily become one in which the author might seek to satisfy the desires of those who enjoy a little social titillation, particularly if spiced up with a tad of scandal – sexual scandal preferably. But such a book might, other than merely feed the perfectly understandable desire to amuse, lack any further real point or purpose. Maymyo certainly had and still does retain many lovely old British colonial properties. Without doubt, those same houses hosted many a drinks party with whisky and gin aplenty, loosening the tongues of some and causing others to blow caution to the wind. Yes, a fun book to write and for many, a fun book to read. But there was more to

Kachin Girls.

A Shan Beauty.

KARENS IN BURMA.

Shan Lady.

Shan woman from Maymyo

Maymyo than that. There was something about Maymyo and the Shan hills, something very difficult to define, hard to put your finger on, which attracted extremely interesting people, gifted people, unusual people, odd people even. It attracted people who wanted to do or already had achieved particularly useful deeds in their lifetime; people who wished to continue their quest because they knew that life and health were not forever, but merely fleeting moments. As Somerset Maugham described it in *'The Painted Veil'* while some of our featured characters were alive: *'a little smoke, lost in the air, that was the life of man'*.

What was it that attracted these types to Maymyo – the temperature maybe? Not really – all hill stations delighted in their cool and temperate climates; that is why they were there. The glorious natural beauty of the Shan hills perhaps? Again, probably not; the views from Cambodia's Bokor go on seemingly forever and the gorgeous jungle and exotic flora and fauna surrounding Penang's Crag are beyond exuberant. Perhaps it was the overall 'package' as it would be described these days; the cool and balmy evenings, those 'murmuring' hills, relatively easy access to Mandalay and hence to onward rail and river communications to Rangoon. It attracted the adventurous for its exciting remoteness and the gentleness of the Shan people amongst whom the British would live out much of their lives. All of these things, yes, but what else has made it quite so special and the pull quite so strong? There must have been a certain 'something' in the Shan hills air; goodness knows what, but it drew people in and made many stay on, long after their retirement when ordinarily they would have headed back home to England.

Above right: Shan women, Maymyo, 1981
Below right: Children on a veranda. Maymyo, 1981
Left: Shan woman from Maymyo, c.1900

Whilst Maymyo charmed many, it still could not keep its hold on some. It is said that George Orwell was one who delighted in the town, but who certainly was not one inspired to remain. A former Irish Guards officer by the name of Bryham, horribly mutilated fighting on the Western Front in the First World War, sought and found solace, not in a remote and gentle corner of Ireland, but near a lake in Burma between Rangoon and the Shan hills where he was to remain for years. And a former Indian Army Officer, Major C.M. Enriques sought the peace and solitude he needed to write, not in Cheltenham or Simla, but in the Shan hills near the town of Mogok. And write he did – several well received histories of Burma and Ceylon and of their peoples. He wrote some charming, Kiplingesque children's books about ponies and some touching if sentimental poetry about dogs. But for all of these very 'different' people, these geographical outliers, Maymyo seemed to be the epicentre. Something about Maymyo and the hills enticed many to stay on well into old age, having extinguished their desire to return 'Home', the hankering for which *'no amount of fog, cold, monotony and dreary oblivion in his English afterlife, ever dispels'*. Pity the repatriates; *'them people from abroad'* as the writer Ruth Bulman put it, who *'try to slake the long years of homesickness which, now they have come home can never be appeased'*. Lucky also, those who loved Maymyo so much that they never could leave.

Former Bombay Burma Trading Company teak-man Gordon Hunt describes in *'Forgotten Land'* something of the magic of the place: *'Maymyo in those days was perhaps one of the loveliest hill stations in the whole Far East. It was only an hour's drive from Mandalay. True the drive was a tortuous one as one climbed from the dreary plains of the Irrawaddy into a land of rich red soil, rolling hills covered in oaks, gracious houses with gardens rich with colour the year round. Government House, Flagstaff House, a paradise for the privileged, a place where sick men convalesced if they were lucky enough to belong to the right firm. Tourists had never been heard of. Who anyway had heard of Maymyo? The army, the numerous Government departments and the great teak companies had. This was snob Burma. This was where they based themselves in the hot months. The centre was The Club which sprawled and stretched out overlooking polo grounds and the fairways of a golf course maintained to international standards. But all this display of opulence, this Victorian extravaganza was nought compared with what the forestry department had done. Like a complicated necklace of interlaced jewels they had encircled the station with a hundred miles of well-kept rides. There was Lady's Mile, the Five Mile Bottom, Rotten Row, a whole maze of pathways… every yard beautifully kept'.*

The map opposite shows the layout and routes of these many, beautiful rides, all if not emanating from, certainly orbiting around, that social epicentre – The Club.

But it might never have been Maymyo at all – the main hill station that is. The British first considered Taung-gyr to the south as a likely spot, as well as a site in the hills of the gem-mining region of Mogok. However, they decided to establish a smaller hill station, Kalaw, in the hills to the west of Taung-gyr and another at Loi Mwe in the state of Kengtung and it was Maymyo, (then Pyin-u-Lwin), which was chosen to be the principal station. Maymyo was, before the arrival of the British, the seat of a *ne-ok*, (a township officer) under the Government of Ava. The British Army had almost stumbled upon Pyin-u-Lwin, then a small, Danu hill tribe village in 1886 after the capture of Mandalay at the end of the Third Anglo-Burmese War.

As Volume 17 of *'The Imperial Gazetteer of India'* precisely points out, Maymyo, or Pyin-u-Lwin lies at latitude 22°, 2' north and longitude 96°, 28' east on the Lashio-Mandalay trail, 3,500ft up in the Shan hills of Burma, some 440 miles north of Rangoon and forty-two miles east of Mandalay; *'lost in the clouds'* as one wistful former resident described it. Former colonial administrator Maurice Collis was one who succumbed to the call of home, only to return years later to research a book he was commissioned to write on the Shan. His writings from the 1930s relate to the meetings and dinners he had with the *sawbwas* and with their principal

MAYMYO & THE SHAN HILLS

Routes of many beautiful horse rides orbiting around Maymyo

Government House, Maymyo, c.1905

Government House interior, Maymyo, c.1905

wives, or *Mahadevis*. When reading the names of some of the *Mahadevis*: Lady Gliding Foam, Lady Pink Gold, Lady of the Celestial Lotus and Princess Sao Nang Tip Htila of Kengtung, the Lady Ambrosia of Heaven, then the social delicacy of the people and probably the biggest of all draws, the exquisiteness of their manners becomes so evident and attractive. After one such dinner the *Mahadevi* enquires of him *'Chin-wan-yu-hu?'* or, *'have you eaten sweetly?'* As Collis then wrote, *'the Shan aristocracy carry manners to such a point of grace that they become a cult'*. He could think little else of them.

Once in Maymyo, settled and recovered from the earlier fighting, the British Army then readied and prepared itself for the occupation of the Shan States. They could have been forgiven for not rushing off to the States. The rolling hills, gentle climate and the cool evening air in Pyin-u-Lwin reminded the nostalgic and pragmatic British of the hill stations of Simla and of Ootacamund (commonly known as Ooty). So, partly on the recommendation of Colonel Stedman, they established a more permanent military presence, renaming the town Maymyo, or May Town, after Colonel James May of the Rangoon-based 5th Bengal Infantry and Maymyo's first military commander.

By 1900 when the town was connected by rail to Mandalay and thence to Rangoon, it became the summer capital of the British Raj. Henceforth, every year, the Government in Rangoon decamped lock, stock and barrel to Maymyo to escape the enervating monsoon months of the coast and the plains. The military presence – the Burma Division, was largely composed of members of the Indian Army. That is why large Indian, Anglo-Indian and Nepali (from Gurkha Regiments) communities continue to live in harmony with one another and with the Burmans, Kachins, Shans and other ethnic groups in and around the town. In his memoirs *'A Civil Servant in Burma'*, the normally reserved Sir Herbert Thirkell-White, an early Maymyo administrator, spoke of his feelings for Maymyo thus: *'On that plateau … the winter climate is perfect. We rode through forest paths and fairy glades, wild roses clustering the hedges. Pyin-u-Lwin, a charmingly situated village of some five and twenty houses with a market place and a gambling ring won our hearts'.*

Edwin Lutyens believed that architects should *'build as an Englishman dressed for the climate, conscious only that the tailor was of Agra or Benares, not of Savile Row or Petticoat Lane'*. In other words he advocated building in the vernacular to suit local climatic and geographical conditions. But as the British began to build in Maymyo, White thought the town looked and felt *'conspicuously un-oriental, more like a corner of Surrey than of Burma'*, an observation which could have been made of Simla and Ooty in India, Nuwara Eliya in Ceylon and most of the hill stations established by the British in the 20th century – so often did they insist on replicating 'Home'. This was not usually the case at lower altitudes and on the plains, where they had to recognise climatic reality and follow Lutyens' advice and build with tall ceilings, ranks of windows and huge, accommodating verandas. But Surrey-style or in the vernacular, build the British very much did. Within a few years, *The Imperial Gazetteer of India* recorded: *'there were twenty-three miles of metalled roads….a residence for the Lieutenant Governor, a circuit house, the Secretariat and several dâk and inspection bungalows besides offices for the sub-divisional officer and the various officials of the Public Works and Forestry departments'*.

By the turn of the 20th century or shortly afterwards there was an Anglican church, a Catholic church and a Garrison church. There was a Church of England girls' school, a Roman Catholic school, a hospital, a telegraph office, a twenty million-gallon capacity reservoir and inevitably, a club, about whose members and their frequently fatuous rules we shall read later. Then in 1915 forestry officer Alex Rodgers, with the help of others, established that final British seal of both local approval and committed settlement – the Botanic Gardens (now the National Kandawgyi Botanic Gardens). As the *'The Burma Gazetteer'* recorded: *'Maymyo lies at the head of a valley with an area of (many) square miles and is surrounded almost entirely by low hills of which the*

Left: The sawbwas *and his followers*
Above: Colonel James May
Above left: Princess Tip Htila of Kengtung
The Lady Ambrosia of Heaven.

FELICE BEATO

Above left: Maymyo c.1890-95
Left: The Harvey family at Marrick House
Above: The garden at Park View House

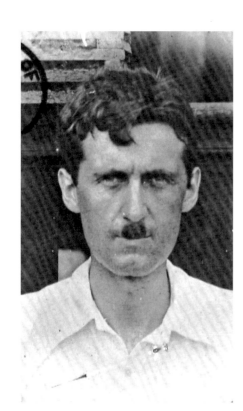

Above: George Orwell
Above right: Tapsy Villa. Family unknown
Right: Russell Square School 1928

Former British bungalow, 1981

Police Training School, Mandalay. Orwell (then Blair) back row, third from the left

highest is One Tree Hill (4,021 feet). The business quarter of the town is at the centre, alongside the Mandalay-Lashio Road and contains a bazaar, Post Office and Telegraph Office. On the outskirts are the residential quarters; British Infantry Lines are on the east and the Indian Infantry Lines on the west. A lake has been made by damming up the southern end of the valley and a Park and Botanical Garden have been laid out round it. An electric light supply has recently been provided. There is a hospital with 74 beds and a Railway Dispensary'. Reasonable progress after just a few decades.

The gentle climate and cool, clean air made the town a fine location for the further establishment of schools. The Government English High Schools office opened St Mary's, St Michael's, St Albert's and St Joseph's schools for the education of children of settlers, administrators and soldiers, thus avoiding the need to send children back to England for their schooling at great cost to both purse and heart.

In the early years of British settlement, administrators led a particularly peripatetic life. By necessity, household furniture was of the 'let's pack up quickly and remove' type, as few stayed in one place for a long period before a posting further up-country or back to Mandalay or Rangoon. Creature comforts were at first few and far between; visitor Beth Ellis quickly tired of a supper often consisting of *'chicken soup followed by chicken accompanied by a side dish of grilled chicken'*. But as the years passed, settlers became exactly that – settled. When Inspector Eric Blair of the Indian Imperial Police was posted to Maymyo in November 1923 having completed his police training in Mandalay, he observed, and as George Orwell, later wrote in *'Homage to Catalonia'* on visiting Maymyo, that: *'It is a rather queer experience. You start off in the tropical atmosphere of an eastern city [Mandalay] – the scorching sunlight, the dusty palms, the smells of fish and spices and garlic, the squashy tropical fruits, the swarming dark-faced human beings – and because you are so used to it you carry this atmosphere intact, so to speak, in your railway carriage. Mentally you are still in Mandalay when the train stops at Maymyo, four thousand feet above sea-level. But in stepping out of the carriage you step into a different hemisphere. Suddenly you are breathing cool sweet air that might be that of England and all round you is green grass, bracken, fir trees and hill women selling baskets of strawberries'.*

By the 1920s it wasn't just strawberries that he could buy with ease. The wine merchants Bernes, Arthur & Co. had opened a store in the town as had Burma Cold Stores, the chemists E.M. de Souza and the general store Apcar Bros. The biggest store to open, and proof of the viability of Maymyo as a commercial centre was Whiteaway, Laidlaw & Co. This was a cash only company, hence its nickname 'Rightaway and Paid For' which, with its forty-seven branches was one of the largest department stores in the Middle and Far East. All in all, Maymyo had become a comfortable place to live. By the mid-1930s over 140 villas or bungalows with names redolent of 'Home' like Camberley, Audrey Villa, The Red House and Lovedale had been built, thus creating an English middle and upper middle-class haven; a vision of heaven for many but for some, a vision of hell.

Maymyo was not fairyland. The town, or rather the British inhabitants, were not all perfect citizens. In a letter to her mother in England, Muriel Bowden, married to a Bombay Burmah employee wrote that outside the Club there were *'chairs on the lawn where all the lads and lasses collect, drink one another's health and strip various wretches of any good reputation they might have'*. The fantasy world in which some British residents of Kalaw lived and which gave Maurice Collis the horrors, could just as easily have been applied to some of the residents of Maymyo. Nor were all visitors to Maymyo enchanted either. In *'Golden Earth'* Norman Lewis, surprised by the over-Anglicisation of the town, as he saw it, felt as if he was *'entering Forest Gate'*. In fairness, he visited Maymyo in the 1950s, when its glory days had waned and while it was still recovering from the ravages of war.

There was a darker side too, not unique to Maymyo, but probably common to all microcosms of transplanted life where emotions run high and people snap – where events suddenly occur. An accomplished and decorated British Army Officer (of whom more later) and resident of Maymyo was murdered there whilst out riding one morning in May 1931. Just a few months later, in August, a newly married assistant military surgeon shot his young wife dead in her bed before lying down by the side of the bed and shooting himself through the mouth.

Things can happen in rarefied places. Some think it's the altitude, others the solitude. These terrible tragedies aside, the rationally critical Collis describes how the majority of the British he met in the Shan States, were so hugely interested in the States, the families, the family trees, the people and in their lives and customs to a degree that he, a highly experienced colonial officer, had not hitherto witnessed. He believed that in general people thoroughly engaged with their home and surroundings, with the people amongst whom they lived and with and to whom they contributed a great deal. It is a selection of these people who are the subjects of this book, some British, some Burmese in equal measure. These were people who really lived their lives to the full. Not for them a life of the prosaic. They grasped the opportunity to make constructive contributions or made adventurous and exciting discoveries, while they had the chance before, ultimately and inexorably, *anno domini* led them quietly and unnoticed into a provincial obscurity where all that remains are memories. The past recedes, fading into hazy fragments of those memories and the happy, endless days of immortal youth, for all of us, simply wither away. But having *lived* – when old, retired and with their best days gone, not for these people regret; not for them the hourly clatter of the kettle being put on the hob to fill time, nor the pitiful sound of old men silently crying for lost youth and wasted years.

Maymyo Street Scene, Maymyo

Maymyo Club, Maymyo

Maymyo Barracks, Maymyo

'To be lifted from the airless plain into the soft breezes and cool air of the hills breathed new life into us all.'

Susan Williams, wife of 'Elephant Bill'

The Forest Men

During the 'British Time', Burma became known by many as the Scottish Colony. Somerset Maugham referred to it as such in *Gentleman in the Parlour*, after travelling through the country in the 1920s. Visitors to Rangoon recorded in their diaries that to them, being in Rangoon felt oddly akin to being in Glasgow, but with much nicer weather! It is difficult to ascertain as to precisely why it should have been the Scots rather than the English, Irish or Welsh who so dominated the Burmese economy. However, at that time, Burma needed the expertise of engineers and shipbuilders to compete on the world stage; Scotland and Glasgow in particular, offered both. Even so, the domination of mercantile British colonial Burma by the Scots is remarkable.

The Scots had a zest for empire travel and the volume of work undertaken by them was also disproportionately high in India, Malaya, Sarawak and Hong Kong as well. Jardine Matheson for example, that great Hong Kong *'Hong'* is a Scottish founded company as is Hong Kong's premier bank, The Hong Kong & Shanghai Banking Corporation. Further south-west in Malaya the rubber estate owner and manager of Guthrie & Co. was Scottish, as was the Sime half of its great competitor Sime Darby. Further west the Bengal jute business was controlled and managed by Scots from Dundee, and St Andrew's Societies existed in almost every large city colonised or controlled by the British. The Scots would most likely put this all down to being the sons and daughters of Adam Smith. The less charitable might put it down to relatively limited opportunities in Scotland combined with the Caledonian weather.

For whatever the reason, in Burma the roll call of Scottish companies was extraordinary. One of the first firms to set up in Burma was D. Shaw & Co. of Glasgow, a supplier to the teak industry. Bulloch Bros., a major rice exporter was also Scottish and its rice milling engines were built by Cowie Bros. in Glasgow. Bulloch's main competitor in the rice milling business was Steel Bros. Another Glasgow company founded William Strang Steel in the 1870s. Burmah Oil grew out of David Sime Cargill's Rangoon Oil Co. with headquarters in Glasgow. Much of the equipment for the oilfields, railways, and the river boats themselves was manufactured in Glasgow and shipped out, usually, on a P. Henderson ship from the port of Glasgow. The arrangements for the shipping and the insurance of the goods would most likely have been made through J&F Graham & Co. with offices in Grahams Building, Rangoon and, yes, in Glasgow. What about the specialist steam trains required to pull carriages up the steep and tricky gradients to Maymyo? They were built by Dunn & Co. in Glasgow. And already mentioned in the preceding chapter, the main department store in Burma, Whiteaway & Laidlaw was also Scottish.

The connection between Burma and Scotland was so strong and trade so extensive that companies usually had offices in Glasgow and Rangoon. Sometimes companies employed the same architect to design or at least advise on the buildings in both countries. This led some people, from the 1870s onwards, to see a similarity in the architecture of the two cities, making them feel quite at home in both places. Scotsman John Begg who trained under the Gothic revivalist Hippolyte Blanc and who developed the then popular Indo-Saracenic style of architecture and Thomas Oliphant Foster are, to the architectural student, the most obvious examples of the people then building Rangoon. But their Saxon counterparts, Henry Hoyne-Fox, Charles Stevens and James Ransom deserve a mention too, given their contributions to the built environment of the city.

And what about the grid system plan and the general layout of the city of Rangoon? That was by Alexander Fraser, a Captain of the Royal Engineers. Should Fraser have had to travel across the Gulf of Martaban from Rangoon to Moulmein or Tavoy or up the coast to Akyab he would most likely have taken a paddle steamer of the Calcutta & Burma Steam Navigation Co. (later the British India Steam Navigation Co.) founded by William MacKinnon in 1856 in Glasgow. When in a hurry he would have taken either the 'Ramapura' or the 'Rasmara', fast paddle steamers, both built

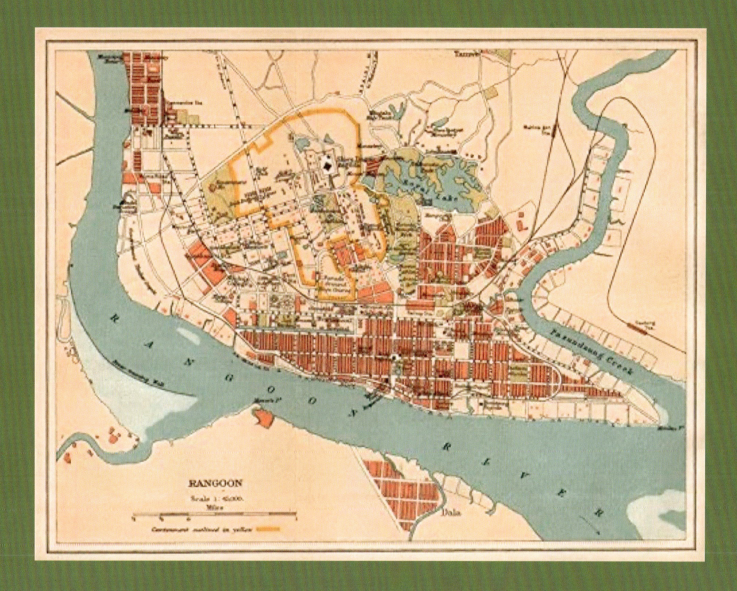

in Scotland. These two fast steamers were known in the Gulf as *Pan-ma-Hyno* or 'before the flowers fade', meaning that a girl in Rangoon could deck her hair with flowers in the morning and reach Moulmein before the flowers had faded.

Many of the British companies operating in Burma were efficient and successful, more than a few of which existed for seventy or eighty years until nationalisation took over in the late 1940s. One of the biggest and most successful of these companies and one which was vital to the administration and to the economic growth of the country was the near legendary and romantically named Irrawaddy Flotilla Co. (IFC). Its origins date back to 1852 when four paddle steamers of the Bengal Marine were sent to Burma to assist in the prosecution of the 2nd Anglo-Burmese War. After the war had ended in 1864 the Chief Commissioner, Colonel Arthur Phayre, correctly concluded that the State should not be involved in the business of enterprise. So, he decided to offer the four steamers and three flats (barges) for sale to private enterprise, with a five-year contract to run mails, stores and people along the 250 river miles between Rangoon and Thayetmyo. Local firm Todd, Findlay & Co. based in the three ports of Rangoon, Moulmein and Akyab bid for the steamers and for the contract, winning it with a price then, of £16,200 or Rs162,000.

Many of the steamers' Bengal marine officers and their Chittagonian lascar crews transferred to the new service, allowing Todd & Findlay to commence operations almost immediately. However, Todd & Findlay was a good, but small agency, and at that stage in its development not quite substantial enough to handle what was a big and growing business. Realising this, the general manager James Todd turned to Thomas Findlay, senior partner in Glasgow who, along with Dumbarton shipbuilder Peter Denny and James Galbraith of Patrick Henderson and Co. of Glasgow (known as Paddy Henderson's) formed a syndicate to take over the contract. The new company, the Irrawaddy Flotilla & Burmese Steam Navigation Co. took over operations on 1 January 1865.

James Galbraith's thinking was clear; the IFC would piggy back off the Henderson Line's exports shipping business by cross-loading goods exported from the UK on Henderson ships landing in Rangoon. Transportation of the goods would continue up the Irrawaddy for sale by local trading houses in the many towns and trading halts out in the *mofussil* (regions) on the way up to Mandalay. The syndicate formed by Denny, Galbraith & Todd was in a far stronger position to raise capital. Therefore new steamers were built and by 1868 the IFC was running fortnightly services the 597 miles up to Mandalay. The majority of IFC steamers (640 at one point) were built in Scotland on the Clyde, crated up in sections, then sent to Mandalay and Rangoon for assembly, making it the largest river fleet in the world.

Early in 1881 the general manager of the IFC Charles Kennedy, went on an expedition up the Chindwin river in the north to ascertain whether there might be commercially viable demand for steamer traffic that far up-country.

The Royal Hotel, Rangoon, at 619 Merchant Street.
Its first owner was J.W. Darwood, a man of Scottish descent.
He also built the Strand Hotel and the Rangoon tramway

Above: The Presbyterian Church (Scots Kirk) was established in Rangoon in 1873 through the efforts of the Reverend G. Fordyce

Above right: Sir Robert Laidlaw, founder of Whiteaway & Laidlaw

Right: The Strand Hotel, Rangoon, opened in 1901

A Henderson Line vessel steaming into Rangoon from Liverpool

IFC stern wheeler on the Chindwin river

THE IRRAWADDY FLOTILLA
AND
BURMESE STEAM NAVIGATION COMPANY,
(LIMITED)

Incorporated under "The Companies' Act, 1862" by which the Liability of each Shareholder is limited to the amount of his Shares.

CAPITAL £100,000—in 2,000 SHARES of £50 Each.

FIRST ISSUE £60,000 IN 1,200 SHARES OF £50 EACH, OF WHICH £30 PER SHARE IS AT ONCE TO BE CALLED UP.

Further Calls will be made as required for the purposes of the COMPANY, at intervals of not less than Three Months from the date of any previous Call.

DIRECTORS:
T.D. FINDLAY, ESQ. (MESSRS. T.D. FINDLAY & CO.), GLASGOW.
PETER DENNY, ESQ. (MESSRS. WILLIAM DENNY & BROTHERS), Dumbarton.
ROBERT HENDERSON, ESQ. (MESSRS. P. HENDERSON & CO.), Glasgow.
WILLIAM DAVIE, ESQ. (MESSRS. J.J. MUIR & DAVIE), Glasgow.
JAMES NICOL FLEMING, ESQ., MERCHANT, Glasgow.
JOHN M'AUSLAND, ESQ. (MESSRS. DENNY & CO.), Dumbarton.
JAMES GALBRAITH, ESQ. (MESSRS. P. HENDERSON & CO.), Glasgow

BANKERS:
THE CLYDESDALE BANKING COMPANY, GLASGOW.

SOLICITORS:
MESSRS. MOODY, M'CLURE, & HANNAY, GLASGOW.

AGENTS AT RANGOON, MAULMAIN, AND BASSEIN:
MESSRS. TODD, FINDLAY, & CO.

OFFICES AT GLASGOW:
15 ST. VINCENT PLACE.

Former Irrawaddy Flotilla Company offices, Rangoon

Drawing of various types of vessel plying the Chindwin river

Yenangyaung (stream of oil) oil wells, 1920s. Oil has been extracted here since the mid-18th century

Raft of teak logs on the Irrawaddy, waiting to be released downriver

He was accompanied by Annan Bryce, general manager of the Bombay Burmah Trading Corporation (BBTC) who needed to survey teak concessions on the Upper Chindwin that the BBTC had secured a year earlier. The trip was long and arduous, but was a great success. Kennedy concluded that a service between the towns of Pakokku and Kindat on the Upper Chindwin river was indeed viable and duly ordered the required shallow drafted stern-wheelers from Dennys on the Clyde. Furthermore, Bryce's tour of the teak concessions confirmed to him that they were as valuable as he had been led to believe – even more so, given the rapidly increasing demand for teak. One of the added benefits for the IFC from this successful joint trip was that shortly afterwards the company was awarded lengthy contracts to carry various BBTC products and its staff along the river which they continued to do for another sixty years. 1886 saw the formation of the Burmah Oil Co. and within a few years the IFC was carrying oil in barges from Yenangyaung to Rangoon for both domestic Rangoon use and onward shipment to India.

Teak *(Tectona grandis)* was at this time a core component of Burma's economy. Both Burma and Siam were blessed with huge growths of teak. However, the trees were not easy to access and seldom, if ever, grew in teak groves or stands; they intermingled with other trees throughout the jungle. Worldwide demand for this extraordinary, hard-to-procure wood was huge. Teak is a unique wood. The trees grow to a height of 130 feet (40 metres), the wood is immensely dense and therefore heavy – on average 40lbs per cubic foot and it is resistant to termites and decay. Its density and its high silica content permit it to withstand extremes of temperature without materially measurable expansion or contraction. Teak can remain wet or even submerged in water for years and yet still not succumb to any form of rot.

Right: Cutting teak in a Burma forest, 1920s

Candacraig, 1981

When the Ava Bridge was built in 1934, teak foundations from an earlier bridge were discovered in the river and had to be removed. When sent for examination and ageing by arboreal scientists, it was estimated that this teak piling was several hundred years old. Despite having been underwater all that time, the teak was still almost rock hard. Teak was used extensively in boatbuilding, from small, expensive pleasure craft to medium size coastal traders. It was used in the manufacture of furniture until it became prohibitively expensive; then it was used to create veneers to 'dress' the exterior of furniture constructed of lesser wood. It was used to deck ships of the Royal Navy and it was the wood of choice for the construction of domestic houses in the Far East. At one point, Burma produced 75% of the world's teak and the company with the lion's share of teak concessions was the Bombay Burmah Trading Corporation (BBTC). The origins of the BBTC lay in Scotland at the firm of Wallace Brothers, a London-based trading house founded in 1863 by two of the six sons of Edinburgh architect Lewis Alexander Wallace. Via another family company, Wallace and Co. in Bombay, the BBTC was established and then floated on the stock market in Bombay *'to carry on trade with and at Burmah and its neighbouring countries'* as its original memorandum of association made clear.

Candacraig, 1981. Hall and staircase

The 173-mile Mandalay to Lashio road runs north-east from Mandalay towards its destination in the Shan hills, passing through Maymyo. Follow the road through the middle of town, turn south along the Circular Road until you are half way to the Botanic Gardens, turn left, eastwards towards East Ridge and you see, tucked away on the Anawrahta Road, an extraordinary house. You might think it an apparition, a building that appears to have drifted away from Scotland, got lost, shrugged its shoulders at its navigational error and gently settled and been forgotten. This is the Candacraig Hotel. It nestles among its Scottish architectural and spiritual siblings: Burnside, Pinehurst, Ranelagh and Rossendale. It has been a hotel since the 1940s, at times part-privately owned, sometimes state owned, at times open and operating and at times not. But it was not always a hotel.

During the British time, not only in Burma, but also in other colonies, British companies established what the army called a Mess and what companies called Chummeries. Hong Kong & Shanghai Bank had one in Hong Kong even into the 1990s. A chummery (all chums together) was the name given to the bachelors' quarters, a building provided by the company where younger and unmarried employees could live together as in an Army Officers' Mess. It comprised private bedrooms, with shared dining and entertaining rooms, and in the early days at least, a lot of rules as to dress and conduct. As time went by and as societal strictures eased, looser definitions and less rigidly defined usage of the building developed. A chummery could also be a large, usually an impressively smart and fashionable house located in a hill station. Here the unmarried and later, the married, could go on leave for a weekend or longer at what was fast becoming a sort of corporate holiday home. In the case of Maymyo, a relaxation of rules was made easier with the construction in 1916 of several separate, private bungalows for their forest officers.

The Candacraig was the Bombay Burmah's chummery. Built in 1904, it took its name from the spectacular 19th century Candacraig House, a Scottish baronial hall lying in the Don valley fifty miles west of Aberdeen, owned by the Wallace family until 1980. The house comprises turrets, gables, verandas, covered porches, sweeping cantilevered staircases, tall ceilings, ivy and trellises; the scent of Scotland and Empire still pervades the building. Here, to the Candacraig came the men from the BBTC. (In those early days it was almost exclusively men). They came for weekends of golf, riding, tennis, cricket, parties, excessive drinking and letting their hair down. They would also come, perhaps for months, to recuperate from disease – dengue fever, typhus, dysentery and cholera, but more often than not, malaria. To the men of the Bombay Burmah, the Candacraig and Maymyo itself became havens of rest. Few published memoirs by Bombay Burmah men remain, but of those which do, most regarded Maymyo as a sanctuary or retreat for when work, heat and solitude took their toll. If only walls could talk; then just sit quietly one afternoon in the Candacraig – and listen.

Whilst these privileged men often had staff to help them with menial tasks, chores and domestic arrangements, the working lives that forest men led whilst away on duty could be very tough indeed – tough and very lonely. Many newly

THE FOREST MEN

THE FOREST MEN

Elephants loading teak

recruited forest officers did not last their first season, finding the climate too harsh. Over the years it was loneliness which accounted for many; spending months on their own was too much for some and resignations were not uncommon. Some were not up to the exacting and taxing demands of the job and were simply, but usually kindly, 'let go'. Even suicides, whilst rare, were not unheard of. Of the forty-one apprentice forest officers who joined in James Williams' intake of 1920, only sixteen remained seven years later.

They were there to work not play, as was made quite clear on joining to a colleague of the author Gordon Hunt by the Rangoon based BBTC managing director. The Big Man had concluded his welcome talk with, in his richest Glasgow accent (an excessive richness employed perhaps for emphasis), the words *'Remember this young man, ye're here to work and not to be a social success'*. The responsibility these men carried at an early age was huge. In *Forgotten Land* Gordon Hunt describes how his senior, a man in his early forties, was responsible for commercial logging operations over a huge area. It was in square miles the equivalent to all of England south of the Thames from Southend in the east to the Bristol Channel in the west. The men were expected to familiarise themselves intimately with their 'patch' and to know, understand and care for the many hundreds of Burmese in their employ. They needed to accumulate more than a rudimentary knowledge of logging, related engines and machinery and, crucially, gain a working knowledge of elephants, their habits, their health, their capabilities and most importantly what tasks they could or should not be required to undertake.

Apart from a few quinine tablets medical provision was practically nil, and whilst a nasty bout of malaria might be survivable, dengue fever, cholera (in early days) or a burst appendix in the forests, often spelt death. The risks and the loneliness were combined with a high degree of commercial and professional responsibility. If one was to girdle (ring bark) the wrong tree for example, a valuable tree might be lost at substantial opportunity cost. Weeks and months away in the forests inevitably led to some of the men falling victim to melancholy. This often led to drinking, which in turn affected their work. The usual cure was several months of leave, sometimes back in England, but often at a retreat to the cool of the Shan hills and Maymyo, which became for many, a second home, a sanctuary from the forests when the forests became so 'dark' that they needed an escape.

The forest men were tough – they had to be to survive, they were resourceful and highly competent. Easy of course to say, glib even, but they really were a different breed. The earlier mentioned James Howard Williams, 'Elephant Bill' as he was known, was not unusual amongst the 'types' to be found within the ranks of the Bombay Burmah. He was a man for whom Maymyo became the happiest and most settled place in which he and his family lived and where they found contentment in all aspects of their lives.

Unusually for the company he was, in fact, not Scottish, but came from Cornwall, the other end of the country. When Williams joined the BBTC in 1920 he may have been a novice to the forests, but he was no novice to life, or more accurately, to death, having spent three years of his young life fighting in the First World War. Williams finished his schooling at Queen's College Taunton in 1915 and only a few months later at the age of eighteen was commissioned into the Devonshire Regiment. He saw action in North Africa, the Middle East and the north-west frontier in India. It was statistically unlikely for an infantry officer to survive three years of front-line service in the First World War, but survive he did and he left the army in the rank of captain in January 1920. He had heard of the BBTC through an old army friend and learned that they were recruiting, their ranks having been depleted on the western front during the war. Of the many who had left the company and travelled to England to join the army, thirteen were killed. In both wars combined, fifteen Military Crosses and three Distinguished Service Orders were awarded to BBTC men. Travel was in Williams' family's blood. His father had travelled the world when young and both of his brothers were already working in India. He applied to the BBTC, was interviewed and accepted and in September 1920, with a one-year letter of engagement tucked in his back pocket, he sailed for Burma on the Henderson Line's *SS Bhamo*.

Part of Williams' war service had been with the Sudan Camel Corps. He had a natural empathy with those difficult, stubborn but magnificent creatures and he hoped to develop a similar affinity with the Asian elephant, an animal crucial to the operations of a logging company. He had read *Notes on Elephants and Their Care* by William Hepburn, the standard work of the day on elephants and their welfare.

Upon arrival at his first posting on the Chindwin river he witnessed a dozen being paraded in front of his boss for inspection. He fell immediately under the spell of these extraordinary, powerful, intelligent and sensitive creatures. 'Elephant' Bill's career path and expertise were henceforth defined. In the first year of his 'apprenticeship' he was sent to the Myittha Valley with responsibility for commercial logging operations over an area the size of an English county. Here he would manage the lives and employment of 300 men and 100 elephants. This degree of responsibility was not of course awarded uniquely to Williams, but to all Assistant Forest Officers at this stage of their careers with BBTC. So, the forests, the teak, the elephants and their uzis (handlers) were to be their lives for as long as they stayed with the company and in the case of Williams it would be for the next twenty years.

The first five or six years of his life with the company was largely spent in the forests. Occasionally, he took leave in Maymyo and Rangoon, but it was in the forests where he lived and worked. He fell victim to the usual variety of jungle diseases which people in his line of work simply accepted as being an unavoidable part of the job and he survived the particularly heavy torrential monsoons of 1927. However, he was weakened badly by 'elephant itch', a fungal fever that leaves suppurating sores on the legs and seriously swollen glands. Even as the itch wore off, malaria came

after him too. In the following year he was promoted to Forest Officer based out of Pyinmana, a logging town about 230 miles north of Rangoon where there were a number of Assistant Forest Officers to help him manage the huge territory for which he was now responsible.

By 1931 Williams, now aged thirty-three, and with eleven years spent in the forests, was just beginning to tire of his own company. The loneliness of the forest was getting to him as it got to most of them at some point in their careers. He began to consider marriage, but finding a wife was a perennial problem for those serving up country and away from the city. The much maligned 'Fishing Fleet', namely young women who came to stay with family in the Far East in the hope of finding a husband, offered opportunity to find a wife for those who worked in the city. However, the competition could be fierce and the results unsatisfactory as described by Rodway Swinhoe in *Phyllis, A Tale from Rangoon*. In fairness to the women, we need to remember that the First World War had slaughtered nearly 750,000 British soldiers, almost exclusively those of marriageable age.

Phyllis was an import new, by the Bibby liner,
Ne'er were eyes such heavenly blue, ne'er was smile diviner,
Mouth demurely arched above, Jim and Jack both fell in love.

Of course, somebody had to win which meant somebody had to lose and when Jack wins Phyllis's heart:
Jim took all his hard-earned pelf, tied it round his body,
Went away and drowned himself in the Irrawaddy.

But for those more or less permanently working out in the remote areas, the 'Fleet' may as well have been moored up in England. It was purely by chance, while out in the forest, he met the Chief Conservator of Forests, Stephen Hopwood. Ordinarily, Hopwood was based in Rangoon, but he was now out touring a number of forest areas. A man in his fifties, Hopwood had spent most of his life in Burma, save for war service in the Royal Artillery, during which time he had won a Military Cross. Returning to Burma after the war,

BURMA.—Waiting for the Steamer.

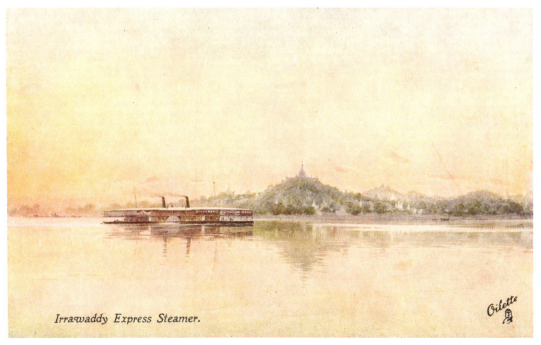

Irrawaddy Express Steamer.

he lost his beloved wife Helen to fever and descended into a depression from which he never fully emerged. He needed a 'chatelaine' to run his house in Rangoon, so he called on his family to send out a niece every now and then to help him. It was 1933 and that niece was Susan Rowland. Williams met her one day at a jungle camp while she was out with her uncle on a journey into the forest. An account of their courtship is superfluous to both the theme and thrust of this book, so suffice to say that their attraction was mutual and Susan accepted his later proposal of marriage. They sailed to England on the Bibby Line's SS *Shropshire* in May 1932 and were married in September in Evesham in the Cotswolds.

By mid-October Jim and Susan had returned and headed for Mawlaik in Upper Burma on the Upper Chindwin river. After little more than a year Jim was given a new job in Shwebo, near Mandalay, where they were to remain until the war. They had visited Maymyo before, but in the summer of 1939 the family decamped there seemingly on a full-time basis and Susan fell in love with the town: *'to be lifted from the airless plain into the soft breezes and cool air of the hills breathed new life into us all'* she wrote. By now they had a son, Treve. Jim's brother Tom, who lived in India and had recently lost his wife to disease, sent his two children to live with Jim and Susan in Maymyo. They had an idyllic two and a half years as an extended family of five in the cool of the hills and whilst Jim genuinely loved jungle life and Susan loved to be with him on his treks, nevertheless it seems clear that their time in Maymyo was the golden period of their lives. Here, the war seemed further away than ever. It was as if Maymyo was a cocoon, insulating and protecting them from the looming realities of war.

Late in 1941 the clouds of war in the East were gathering. Even the most optimistic, even those who simply could not force themselves to conceive of yet another war so soon after the horrors of the last, could sense this next war coming ever closer. In November 1941 and with either fortuitous timing or uncanny foresight, Tom Williams arrived in Maymyo to collect his children and take them back to India.

He suggested that Susan and Treve come with him too, but Susan insisted that she would stay with her husband. One month later the Japanese bombed Rangoon.

With the Japanese army already on Burmese soil and the British Army about to begin the long, exhausting and costly retreat north, Jim Williams, a man of oft-demonstrated fortitude and ability, rose again to the most extraordinary series of challenges. In early January a telegram arrived ordering the family to go to Mandalay. A few days later the company ordered the evacuation of the wives and children of all of its employees. Williams was ordered to escort a group of around fifty evacuees north to Mawlaik on the Chindwin, an area they knew well, it being their first married posting back in 1933. From there the plan was to move on foot to Manipur in India, over 140 miles away. Williams knew well the enormity of such a trek and whilst he realised that the young and the fit might make it, it could prove to be impossible for many of the women and children. The answer was immediately obvious to Jim Williams and his old company friend Geoff Bostock – elephants! And so, on 23 February 1942 nearly seventy women and children and sixty elephants set out from Mawlaik heading for Manipur. Everybody walked including the women and children, while the elephants carried indispensable supplies of food, water and tentage. From Tamu near the Indian border they crossed some daunting ridges, then dropped down to the hot plains. At last they reached Palel in Manipur and were taken in trucks to Dinapur, their destination. This is where Jim said goodbye to his wife and son and returned to Burma where he needed to make arrangements for the elephant, Bandoola, the famous huge tusker, to be led into the deepest, most remote parts of the forest with his uzi Po Toke. This was to ensure the Japanese did not get hold this magnificent beast and use him as part of their war machine or kill him in order to prevent the British from using him again. Once satisfied that Bandoola was safe, he trekked all the way out again, reaching Shillong weeks later, where his family were living with his brother. Williams arrived just in time to witness the birth of his daughter Lamorna.

The army quickly realised that Williams' knowledge of Burma and his fluency in the languages could be of huge value to the war effort, so they awarded him a commission. Thus a man who had fought in the First World War, was again attached to Force 136 (a behind the lines unit) and sent to Tamu where he was to ascertain how many elephants remained of the original numbers that were company elephants. Within days he had gathered over fifty elephants and their uzis and with the help of another old company friend Harold Langton Browne, they mustered well over 1,000 elephants between that point and the end of the war. Then they spent two years giving invaluable service to the Royal Engineers in building bridges and providing elephant power to haul kit and equipment necessary for bridge and road building over terrain which vehicles could not travel. In doing so they made a major contribution to the defeat of the Japanese army in Burma. For his services during the war, Williams, now a Lieutenant Colonel, was awarded an OBE and was twice Mentioned in Despatches. This was the calibre of man that the Bombay Burmah employed.

By 1945 and the end of the war, the world had become a changed place. The past really had become 'a foreign country' and there was to be no triumphant return to Maymyo and to the cottage in which the family had been so happy. Nor for Jim a joyful return to the forests and to his beloved elephants. Independence loomed and the Bombay Burmah was to have no lasting place under British management in an independent Burma, so in 1946 the family sailed away, settling in Cornwall. Yet they never really 'settled' as was so often the case; many repatriates, *'them people from abroad'* just never really could.

The Bibby liner in which 'Elephant Bill' and Susan sailed to England in May 1932

'Burmah apparently is crowded with tigers
and wild elephants of a size and ferocity which
filled me with fear. But as every man on
board appeared to have slain tigers and captured
elephants innumerable and that under
the most surprisingly dangerous circumstances,
I felt I should be well protected'.

Beth Ellis, on board ship bound for Rangoon

The Writer

THE WRITER

Wigan is a moderately sized post-industrial town in the north of England, formerly of Lancashire, now part of the Metropolitan Borough of Greater Manchester. It is a typical example of so many English towns that were radically changed by the industrial revolution. In approximately one hundred years Wigan metamorphosed from a quiet and pretty market town in the midst of a great sheep farming area to become a thriving industrial centre. Then, as the heavy industry declined and the sheep markets were no longer even a memory, the town went into sharp decline.

A Royalist stronghold in the English civil war and a thriving market town for the greater part of its history, Wigan began to develop into a mill town almost immediately after the beginning of the industrial revolution. Its fortunes prospered – well, certainly for the mill owners and members of the middle classes. Prosperity continued into the new century until the First World War killed or maimed most of its young men and consequently, the spirits of its widows and mothers. Come the Great Depression the economic doldrums had hit Wigan and by the end of the Second World War the town had slipped into a steady and continuing economic decline as foreign competition and changing tastes hollowed out demand for goods which the town produced. Following its brief industrial interregnum, there was no going back to that quiet, pretty Lancashire market town and Wigan simply declined. Its worthy inhabitants went about their daily business watched over by many grand, sturdy but long-empty mills, a brooding, nagging reminder of the town's industrial past. Strange that this decent, inoffensive yet inconspicuous town should figure, however indirectly, in distant Maymyo's history not once but twice. Perhaps there really is *'something about Wigan'* as one of its less inspired civic advertising slogans once put it.

The Depression of the early 1930s hit not only Wigan. In most English manufacturing towns high unemployment rates, falling wages and a basic welfare system resulted in grinding poverty and appalling living conditions for many. Led by J.B. Priestley who recorded his observations in *English Journey*, several of the country's left-wing literati set out on the northern 'tramp' to see for themselves just how bad conditions were before writing about them.

In 1933, former Burma policeman, writer and one-time Maymyo resident Eric Blair wrote a similar commentary based upon his own observations of urban poverty in *Down and Out in Paris and London* published under his newly created pen name George Orwell; a name dreamt up for him by his publisher Victor Gollancz. He continued this theme of social observation and comment by going north on the 'tramp' himself. He visited Liverpool, Sheffield, Barnsley and then Wigan. Why Wigan? Yes, it was poor, but there were much poorer towns in the north, all hammered by the Depression. For example, the collapse in demand for shipbuilding meant that the towns of Jarrow, Sunderland and Middlesbrough became synonymous with poverty. But no, Orwell went to Wigan. He lived there for over a month, later writing of his observations in *The Road to Wigan Pier*, a grim account of living standards and working conditions of the poor in the soon-to-become post-industrial Wigan. In fact, there was no pier, rather a wharf on the Leeds and Liverpool canal. But again, why Wigan?

As we know Wigan had been a thriving market town for much of its existence, then a boom town during England's heavy industrial period – and then decline. Yet industry and commerce were not the sum total of Wigan's achievements. The town also spawned some important people in the world of the arts including the fêted Victorian Shakespearean actor Jonathan Dewhurst, the operatic tenor Tom Burke, the wildly fashionable modernist artist Christopher Isherwood, the illustrator George Worsley Adamson and the acclaimed L.S. Lowry contemporary Theodore Major. Is it too fanciful to think that Orwell the writer, drawn to Wigan through its poverty and deprivation, may also have been subliminally drawn towards a town which produced such creative talent? There is no evidence to suggest that this may have been the case, so yes, perhaps it is too much of a stretch, too hopeful

THE WRITER

Beth Ellis

Halliwick Manor in Friern Barnet, Middlesex, the school that Beth and her sisters Mary (May), Madge, Ruth and Dorothy attended

and too fanciful, however attractive the idea may be. But then…the very thorough Orwell may also have read some of the writing of Beth Ellis.

Beth Ellis was born in Wigan on 17 September 1874, the fourth of eight children born to Thomas and Mary Ellis. Thomas Ellis was a successful solicitor who went on to become Secretary to the Mining Association and one of the leading mining lawyers in the country. In George V's Coronation Honours list, he was knighted for services to the mining industry. Ellis' professional success ensured that the family were financially well off; they lived in a substantial house called 'The Hollies' on Wigan Lane. Ellis was a great believer in education and sent his three sons to be educated at Rugby and his five daughters to Halliwick Manor school in Friern Barnet, Middlesex.

Beth clearly excelled at her schooling and won a place at Oxford University to read English Literature, arriving at Lady Margaret Hall only a few days after her eighteenth birthday. Women had only been allowed to attend lectures at Oxford since 1879, the date of the founding of Lady Margaret Hall. She was one of forty-one undergraduates when she took up residence there in 1892. As Miles Ellis points out in his short history of his great-aunt Beth, the admission of women to lectures and exams was still a matter of considerable controversy at the time. This is evident from the comments made by John Burgon, the antediluvian Dean of Chichester in his address to New College in 1884, in which he said, that women *'should remain modest mothers in their secret innocence of Physical Sciences and of a creedless philosophy'*. However, the discrimination did not end there. At that time the award of a degree was contingent upon students completing various preliminary courses such as Philosophy, the study of which was not open to women at Oxford; 'Catch 22' as this situation would later be known. Beth was awarded first-class honours in her final exam in English, although she was unable to receive her degree. It would be another twenty-five years, in May 1925, before women were permitted to graduate with an Oxford degree.

Her sister May's marriage to Geoffrey Dawson at their local church, St Michael's, in Wigan in the summer of 1896 led indirectly to Beth's writing career. Geoffrey was a member of the 'Heaven Born' – the Indian Civil Service (ICS) and was stationed in Rangoon to where he and his bride sailed shortly after the wedding.

Their first and only child, Anita Mary (always known as Nita) was born in Rangoon in May 1897. Just a few months after the birth, the ICS posted Geoffrey from Rangoon to Maymyo in the Shan hills. The family soon moved up to the hills into what must have seemed to be a heavenly climate after the sultry heat and humidity of Rangoon. Shortly after her arrival in Maymyo, May sent a letter to her sister Beth in which she asked if she would like to come out to Burma and stay with them. Beth was delighted at the invitation and not in the least daunted by the prospect of an adventurous yet sometimes uncomfortable journey: *'in this matter of fact, little England of ours there are few opportunities outside the yellow backed novel of meeting with real adventures. Picture then my delight when I received an invitation to spend the winter in Burmah. I knew where Burmah was; that it was bounded by Siam, China and Tibet; anything was possible in a country with such surroundings. I was charmed to go'*.

She prepared herself quickly and sailed from Liverpool in November 1897. Fortunately for us, she made copious notes on the outward voyage and maintained a diary whilst staying in Burma. It was only at the end of her stay in Burma, when challenged by a fellow guest at dinner one evening, that she decided to write a book about her journey. Her first book, written the following year and published in 1899 by R. Platt of Wigan, was inspired by her time spent in Maymyo with Geoffrey and May. Some say it was her best book, but it laboured under the lengthy title of *An English Girl's First Impressions of Burmah* – the book hereinafter referred to as 'AEGFIB'. It is a wonderful piece of travel writing which differentiates itself from so many other such writings of the day. Firstly, Beth makes no attempt to use the book as a means of self-aggrandisement or self-publicity and secondly,

The Liverpool dockside from where Beth sailed to Rangoon in November 1897

A view of the dock area in Rangoon where Beth disembarked in December 1897

On the look-out as the vessel passes through the Suez Canal

the book is endlessly amusing in that she pokes fun at herself as well as the legion of 'types' she encounters. This is achieved not in an unkind or cruel manner, but in a gently teasing way, that successfully debunks their occasional drivel and pricks their pomposity, without actually humiliating them.

On board the ship to Rangoon she discovered that *'India was created that the Indian [British official] civilian might dwell therein; the rest of mankind was created to admire the Indian Civilian. Something of this sort I had already heard from my brother-in-law, a member of that service, but one does not pay much attention to what brothers-in-law say'*. She learned that *'Burmah is a land where teak grows in order that "The Bombay Burman" may go there and collect it'* and she also learned that *'Ceylon is a country in which dwell the best (and noisiest!) fellows in the world. They have innumerable horse races, eat prawn curry, are prodigiously hospitable and in odd hours, grow tea.'* Again, not in an unkindly way, she teased and laughed at some of the male egos on board; *'Burmah apparently is crowded with tigers and wild elephants of a size and ferocity which filled me with fear. But as every man on board appeared to have slain tigers and captured elephants innumerable and that under the most surprisingly dangerous circumstances I felt I should be well protected.'* She was advised that if chased by an elephant she should climb up some feathery bamboos. When she later came across the said bamboo, she wondered how anyone could possibly climb it at all, but that 'all things are possible to one pursued.'

She adored the outward journey; her excitement at seeing new lands was palpable; *'...the glimpse, though only distant, of new lands, lands which had hitherto been merely geographical or historical names, but which now acquired a new reality and interest'.* The reader can almost scent the Ceylonese air through the pages as she described the *'...beauty of that long line of open coast, the great breakers glittering with a thousand opal tints in the sunlight and beyond them, the dark blue ocean delicately flecked with shimmering white spray stretching away into the shadowy distance.'*

Beth was not keen to remain in Rangoon for too long as it was for her merely a staging post en route to Maymyo. The city seemed to fascinate and repel her in equal measure. She found the heat dreadfully enervating, heat *'such as Shadrech, Meshech and Abednego never dreamed of'*. She found the Gymkhana Club on the Halpin (then pronounced Hairpin) Road was amusing and interesting, but she laughed gently at the European population whom she felt lived only for the Gymkhana and little else. As for the Pegu Club, Beth, as a woman, would not have been permitted to enter, although it was unlikely to have been her 'cup of tea' in any case. Forty years later the mildly eccentric British ex-Army adventurer Roland Raven-Hart did reside at the Pegu prior to his attempt to canoe up the Irrawaddy river to Mandalay. He commented that it was *'...worth a visit in order to see what used to be alive and to study the fossils of Burma'*, accepting as he did, that he would never be allowed back. In Rangoon, Beth found little of the easy friendliness which she found

THE WRITER

"They go about their duties in a stately, leisurely manner, lifting the logs with trunks, tusks and forefeet"

later in Maymyo, presumably because she saw less of it. In those days Rangoon had a reputation for being somewhat cliquey, and on first acquaintance it probably helped in the 'Scottish colony' if you were Scottish yourself or at least worked for one of the many Scottish companies established in the country.

Her description of watching an elephant moving teak is beautiful and full of understanding, resonating with those who have seen these magnificent creatures at work. *'…they go about their duties in a stately, leisurely manner, lifting the logs with trunks, tusks and forefeet; piling them up with a pull here and a push there and then marching to the end of the pile and contemplating the result with their heads on one side, to see if all are straight and firm. And they do all in such a stately, royal manner that they give an air of dignity to the menial work and one comes away with the feeling that to pile teak side by side with an elephant would be an honour worth living for'.*

Beth took the 386-mile train journey from Rangoon to Mandalay, where she was to be met by her brother-in-law for the journey up into the hills to Maymyo. She observed and noted all of her surroundings, including the train, the passengers and the people in the villages past which the train chugged steadily on its way up-country. She wrote with her usual sense of humour and gentleness about what she saw. She mused to herself, thinking that the Burmese standing on the platform and bowing at the train were actually bowing to her, when in fact, they were bowing to a monk in the next-door carriage. She wrote gracefully of *'…pretty Burmese girls coquetting with their admirers as they carried water from the well or chattering and whispering merrily together as they performed their toilet by the stream, decking their hair with flowers and ribbons and donning their delicately coloured "tamelins".'* And she demonstrated an intuitive appreciation of the country's historic traditions when she visited the palace which, *'…though its shrines have been desecrated by the feet of the alien, though its bazaar has become a warehouse for the sale of Birmingham and Manchester imitations, this former stronghold of the King of Burmah still retains its ancient charm'.*

After a month on board a ship and the hot and slow train journey up country to Mandalay, Beth began the final and most uncomfortable leg of the journey, first by cart and then by pony up through the hills to Maymyo. She and her brother-in-law Geoffrey took a *gharry* for the first seventeen miles to the foot of the hills where they were met by ponies on which they continued their journey up to Maymyo.

At the beginning of *'AEGFIB'*, Beth makes clear just how much she dislikes riding. She describes her fear and her incompetence with her usual honesty and courage. This was a time when it was expected that all of a certain class would both sit on a horse well and enjoy doing so – or at least declare that they did. Not Beth; she loathed horses or at least, loathed riding them. The journey began badly with her pony walking backwards before they had advanced even a yard towards Maymyo. Then when the exasperated syce grabbed the reins and led the pony away with Beth sitting astride and hanging on with some effort, the pony decided that even slow was really too fast and almost came to a halt. Her brother-in-law encouraged and cajoled Beth and the pony, but finally gave up in disgust. He galloped ahead and waited for her to catch up – which she did eventually. They spent the night in a *dâk* bungalow where she ate chicken (the first of many) which, before the pot *'wears a harassed, expectant look knowing that the end will overtake him suddenly and without warning'* which of course, it did.

Next morning, rested and refreshed they continued on the final leg of their journey up to Maymyo. Here again she smiled at herself with such refreshing honesty that the reader cannot help but love her for it. She described the solar topee sitting atop her head not gracefully, not elegantly, but like a plum pudding. It stayed that way until such time as it could no longer endure the wobbling and slipped slowly down over her face, blocking out all vision and hanging on to her head by the elastic chin-strap. Beth had no pretensions to equine ability nor to feminine grace at all times and she arrived at her sister's bungalow saddle-sore, tired, covered in red dust and tumbled into the house swearing that she would never ride a Burmese pony again. Beth, it is fair to assume, would have read anything and everything which she could lay her hands upon on the subject of Maymyo. Perhaps through mispronunciation or mis-hearing she referred to Maymyo as Remyo. The town was called Pyin-U-Lwin before the British arrived, then renamed Maymyo; perhaps Maymyo becomes Remyo in a busy, noisy room. Count Étienne Lunet de Lajonquière referred to Remyo in his book *Le Siam et les Siamois* published in 1906, long after the hill station was renamed Maymyo. The passage of time prevents us from discovering the reason; anybody who might have known the answer is now long gone, but something, some clue may turn up in a diary one day. Of course, this is not of huge importance, merely of interest to the addicted.

Beth spent six months living in Maymyo with her sister and brother-in-law. In *'AEGFIB'* she gives us a clear and comprehensive account of the people, the station and the lifestyle, warts and all. Furthermore, she gives her account of life observed through her usual sharp but non-judgemental eye and always with the same wonderful sense of humour, often laughing at herself as much as she does at others. We get a clear picture of the layout of the town as she lists the buildings, The Club, the court house, the post office, the district bungalow and the half dozen (then) bungalows built for the Europeans. It should be remembered that the British loved and depended upon their clubs; there were at least twenty-eight of them in Burma, from the Akyab Club to the Yamethin Club.

Her description of her sister's house, built by an advocate of fresh air, is hilarious. She thought that since no windows actually closed, the walls were full of chinks and all of the rooms had doors leading one to another, it meant that when the wind blew hard, one needed only go to the back garden to find everything which they had suddenly lost. She laughed gently at the men-only club, but nevertheless she means it: *'The Club House at Remyo is a truly imposing edifice perched high on the hill side, standing in a well-kept compound and surrounded by its offices, bungalows and stables. About the interior of the building I must confess ignorance it being an unpardonable offence for any woman to cross the threshold. It may be that it is but a whited sepulchre, the exterior beautiful beyond description, the interior merely emptiness. I cannot tell'.*

And she is cross, very cross indeed that The Ladies Club is little more than a hut tacked on to the side of The Club: *'At the foot of the club house stands a tiny, one-roomed mat hut, the most unpretentious building I ever beheld, universally known by the imposing title of 'The Ladies Club'. Here, two or more ladies of the station nightly assemble for an hour before dinner to read the two-month-old magazines, to search vainly through the shelves of the "library" for a book they have not read more than three times, to discuss the iniquities of the native cook and to pass votes of censure on the male sex for condemning them to such an insignificant building'.* She delighted in the miles of beautiful rides created with such care and professionalism by the forestry department, and the Burmese women that she met *'...who understand the art of dress and blending colours to perfection'.* She loathed the rats in her room which gave *'balls on her dressing table and organised athletic sports on the floor'* and was clearly greatly saddened when she left Maymyo, her description of her return journey being restrained and brief.

Before leaving Maymyo she made an interesting observation of the British stationed there. George Orwell wrote that the first thing which two Englishmen do when sent abroad is to form a club primarily in order to find some common ground on which to snub one another. In Maymyo however, Beth wrote that she found only friendliness, hospitality and kindness: *'...the Anglo Burmans seem to lose entirely that cold and suspicious reserve of strangers of which we are so often justly accused'.* Again, the Maymyo air perhaps. And as she reflects on Burma, *'...misery seemed to have no place in this land of delight but contentment ever reigns and the happy Burman dreams away his life in a paradise of sunshine'.*

Clearly, it is fair to say that Beth's six months in Maymyo were the inspiration for her to become a writer; the Shan

Beth felt that the European population lived only for the Gymkhana and little else

At the time of Beth's visit women were not permitted to enter The Pegu Club

A dâk *bungalow in which Beth spent a night en route to Maymyo. These were government buildings providing free accommodation to officials*

hills' air breathed its way through to her pen. Following the success of *'AEGFIB'* she went on to write several novels, the first of which, *Barbara Winslow: Rebel* was published in 1903 by Edinburgh publisher William Blackwood & Sons. The 1923 silent Hollywood movie entitled *'The Dangerous Maid'* starring Constance Talmadge was based on this book. Beth also wrote a volume of five short stories published in 1905, under the title *Madame, Will You Walk?* One of the five entitled, *Romance of the Pretender* was adapted for the stage under the title *'Mr Jarvis'* and was performed at the Wyndham Theatre in 1911 with Gerald du Maurier taking the lead. She also penned a romantic novel entitled *The Kidnapper* for *The Windsor Magazine* in 1912. A reviewer in *The Bookman* said of her style that *'There is a swing and a cheerfulness in her writing which is particularly attractive'*.

In 1908, aged thirty-four, Beth married barrister Godfrey Baker at her local church in Wigan, with the groom's father, the Reverend Dr. Baker officiating at the service. Anne Catterall, a local historian commented that *'Beth wore a white satin bridal gown, trimmed with lace and wore the same veil that her mother and sisters had previously worn. She carried a bouquet of white lilies and roses which was a gift from the bridegroom and was attended by six bridesmaids. The three adult bridesmaids wore simple empire gowns of white crêpe de chine and black hats lined with pale blue and trimmed with autumn foliage. They carried bouquets of bronze-coloured chrysanthemums and wore pearl brooches. The three children wore white crêpe de chine dresses trimmed with blue ribbon and lace caps and carried posies of lilies of the valley'*.

The couple honeymooned in Cornwall and then went to live in Berkhamsted in Hertfordshire from where Godfrey could commute easily to chambers and to court in London. In her late thirties, Beth became pregnant and knowing the risks associated with such a late pregnancy, must have crossed her fingers and prayed to God every day. But luck was not on her side; in August 1913 she died in childbirth along with her baby, at the young age of thirty-nine.

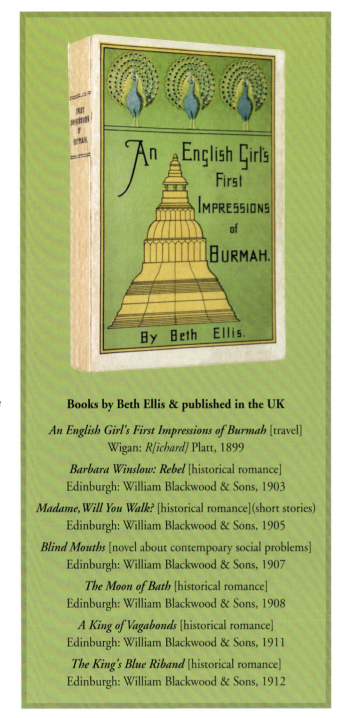

Books by Beth Ellis & published in the UK

An English Girl's First Impressions of Burmah [travel]
Wigan: R[ichard] Platt, 1899

Barbara Winslow: Rebel [historical romance]
Edinburgh: William Blackwood & Sons, 1903

Madame, Will You Walk? [historical romance] (short stories)
Edinburgh: William Blackwood & Sons, 1905

Blind Mouths [novel about contemporary social problems]
Edinburgh: William Blackwood & Sons, 1907

The Moon of Bath [historical romance]
Edinburgh: William Blackwood & Sons, 1908

A King of Vagabonds [historical romance]
Edinburgh: William Blackwood & Sons, 1911

The King's Blue Riband [historical romance]
Edinburgh: William Blackwood & Sons, 1912

'He had the digestion of an ostrich and could do with impunity things which would put most men on the sick list.'

A colleague of Henry Morshead

The Mapmaker

THE MAPMAKER

On Tuesday 19 May 1931, *The Rangoon Gazette* published a statement issued by the Commissioner of Police of the Mandalay Division: *'Shortly after 9 o'clock on the morning of Sunday 17th May, 1931 the Subdivisional Officer, Maymyo, received a telephone message from My Syed Ali of the Maymyo Electric Supply Company to the effect that a riderless pony with blood on its neck and saddle had just come into the compound of his bungalow on Manor House Road from the direction of Elephant Point. He at once collected a dozen policemen and with a Sub-Assistant Surgeon went by car to Mr Syed Ali's house where he found that though the pony was not in any way injured, it was obvious from the large amount of blood upon it that a serious accident had occurred. Meanwhile it has been discovered that the owner of the pony was Lt. Colonel Morshead, DSO, RE, Director of the Burma Circle, Survey of India and that the riderless pony had been seen coming down the hill along Inlya Ride towards Switchback Ride and Elephant Point. As the search along the rides however proved unsuccessful, the Subdivisional Officer, at 12.45pm, telephoned for assistance to the 10th-20th Burma Rifles and parties of them under the direction of the Commanding Officer carefully searched a wide area of jungle to the south of Inlya Ride for the rest of the day, but without success.*

The search was renewed by the Military Authorities at dawn next day and at about 7.30am Captain Briggs, RE, with a party of Dogras discovered Colonel Morshead's body lying in the jungle about 150 yards to the north of Inlya Ride about 2½ miles from Inlya village. A post-mortem examination carried out by the Civil Surgeon, Major McRobert, made it clear that Colonel Morshead had been killed instantaneously by a gunshot fired at very close range into his chest whilst a second shot, fired from a greater distance had made superficial pellet wounds on the back and side of the left shoulder. An examination of the place where the body was found suggested that the shots were actually fired while the Colonel was on the ride and that his pony afterwards carried him into the jungle.'

Henry Morshead had moved with his wife and five children to Maymyo in 1929 to take over the job he had recently been offered as Director, Burma Circle of the Survey of India, an important job with not a small degree of prestige attached to it. He was a regular Army Officer of the Royal Engineers and had only recently been promoted to the rank of Lieutenant Colonel. The family moved into a house called Upperfold, a comfortable, rambling house which stood in a compound of some three acres on the East Ridge a mile or so from the centre of town and from the Survey of India offices.

Morshead was only 47 years old when he and his family went to live in Maymyo and yet he had already achieved in that 47 years more than most might do in several lifetimes. In demeanour and in character he was very much a product of his English type and time.

As a child, Henry Morshead attended Kelly College 'for the sons of naval officers and other gentlemen' on the outskirts of Tavistock in Devon, before proceeding to Winchester College, where he demonstrated a marked aptitude for mathematics, an essential attribute for his work at the Indian Survey. From Winchester he advanced to the Royal Military Academy, Woolwich, and was later to be commissioned into the Royal Engineers. A further two years training followed at the School of Military Engineering in Chatham, after which he and his young fellow officers joined their regiments. Morshead had applied for service in India and through ability and good fortune achieved his aim. He joined the Military Works Department in the United Provinces of Agra and Oudh, now the State of Uttar Pradesh in India, where he became Garrison Engineer. Although vital, the routine nature of his work bored him, so when the opportunity to join the Survey of India arose in 1906, he jumped at it.

The Survey was staffed primarily by officers of the Royal Engineers and it had rightly earned a fine international reputation headquartered in Dehra Dun and its main task was to produce accurate maps of the country, a job which entailed many months of survey work out in the field, an activity well suited to Henry Morshead; he was fit and tough. A colleague said of him that *'he had the digestion of an ostrich and could do with impunity things which would put most men on the sick list.'*

Morshead was a fine professional officer and his work for the Survey was meticulous and thorough. The Survey enjoyed a hard won and jealously guarded international reputation and without doubt many officers in later years owed their ability to map read around obscure and far-flung parts of India and Burma to Henry Morshead and the other officers of the Survey.

Assam, in the northeast of India, had never accepted wholeheartedly the authority of the British Raj. In 1911, Noel Williamson, the political officer stationed in Sadiya in Assam and his colleague Doctor Gregorson were murdered by Abor tribesmen near the village of Kebong. Of the fifty porters who had accompanied them on their expedition through Assam only five returned to barracks to tell the tale. Such slaughter and humiliation were entirely unacceptable to the British and they decided to mount a punitive expedition under the command of General Hamilton Bower, an experienced officer with extensive service in China and India. As the expedition was being prepared, the Viceroy of India Lord Harding,

Major-General Hamilton Bower C.B. (facing) commanding the Abor Field Force talking with Colonel Widdicombe, 114th Mahratta Infantry

ordered that the 600-mile eastern frontier with China, a huge swathe of land stretching from Bhutan to Burma, should be properly mapped. This would enable Foreign Secretary, Sir Henry McMahon, to refer to the maps during the upcoming frontier talks with the Chinese, to ensure that the line of the frontier took account of geographical and tribal facts rather than arbitrary political or national desires.

The Survey of India was commissioned to undertake this project and Morshead, aided by one Captain C.P. Gunter were tasked to map that part of the area which included the large eastern tributaries of the Brahmaputra, the Dibang and the Lohit. Two Indian surveyors, Abdul Hak and Allah Ditta joined them at the Kobo base camp near Sadiya in October 1911. The terrain to be surveyed was tough; ridges up to 17,000 feet and falls in the rivers of over forty feet in the mile, turned the rivers into raging torrents during the rainy season. The team worked at the job for four months. During that time they had only thirty-eight days without rain, yet they were still able to survey 3,370 square miles of terrain; an amazing feat under such unfriendly conditions. Unfortunately however, by the time the cold weather set in, their work was still incomplete necessitating a return to the task the following year.

They regrouped in January 1912 and established a base on Achi Hill at 10,000ft, a place with commanding views of the Matun, Dri and Tangon valleys. As mapping proceeded they realised, with justifiable satisfaction, that they were fixing on peaks, ridges, rivers and valleys, which hitherto had been neither seen nor heard of by Europeans. By May 1912 they had completed the huge and vitally important task bestowed upon them by Harding, so they withdrew to Shillong where the map-makers did their work, based upon the Gunter and Morshead surveys. This survey expedition was followed almost immediately by another into the Tsangpo Gorge and then onwards (without permission), into Tibet.

Morshead accompanied Captain Frederick Bailey of the Indian Army, a man later ranked alongside Livingstone, Speke and Younghusband for his pioneering work and who later recorded the details of the expedition in his book *No Passport to Tibet*. Their extensive 1,700-mile, six-month survey proved that the Tsangpo river in Tibet was not separate from the Upper Brahmaputra river – it was the Upper Brahmaputra. But perhaps the most important outcome, particularly for the writer John Buchan, when he mentioned the expedition in his book *Last Secrets* was that: *'their evidence* [referring to Bailey and Morshead] *may be finally considered to have solved the riddle of how the great river* [the Brahmaputra] *breaks through the highest range on the globe.'* Even in an era of many ground-breaking geographical discoveries, those made by Bailey and Morshead were remarkable.

Morshead then took some leave – the first time he had been back to England in ten years. As soon as he returned to India, he was approached by Major Cecil Rawling of the Somerset Light Infantry who invited him to join an expedition he was planning, to survey and climb Mount Everest in 1916. As events turned out, the First World War put paid to his plans, as it did to Rawling himself; he was killed in action three years later in October 1917 at Passchendaele whilst commanding a brigade. Morshead returned to India at the onset of the war, only to be sent back to the UK to join the 75th Field Company, Royal Engineers, part of the 16th (South Irish) Division in Kilworth, County Cork. In the summer of 1915 his company of Royal Engineers received orders that it was to move to St Omer in France to become part of the Guards Division, shortly thereafter to take part in the dreadful Battle of Loos. This battle cost the British over 12,000 casualties including the life of Rudyard Kipling's only son John, who died aged eighteen during the opening scenes of the encounter. Kipling, almost destroyed by grief at his loss later wrote: *'My son died laughing at some jest, I would I knew what it were, and it might serve me at a time when jests are few.'*

Above: Lieutenant-Colonel Henry Morshead on his appointment Director Burma Circle in 1929

Above right: Evelyn Widdicombe in 1913

Right: Henry and Evie Morshead with their family, Maymyo 1931

Henry Morshead was then transferred to an Engineer Company in 33rd Division and took part in the even more horrendous and costly Battle of the Somme. Surrounded by death and misery, it must have come by way of a relief to receive a letter from his Tsangpo valley colleague Eric Bailey, now back in India after serving in France and Gallipoli, having survived being wounded three times. 18 months later, he was working for the Political Department in India and the Great Game was still in full swing, by now however, with the Bolsheviks as the opposition and not the Czar. Working out of Kashgar, Bailey's first coup was to be recruited by the Bolsheviks to hunt down and possibly kill…himself! Bailey thought this an absolute hoot and howled with laughter when recounting the story to Morshead years later. Morshead took a week's leave in October 1916, during which time he met and later married Evelyn Templer Widdicombe (Evie), an Englishwoman who had spent much of her life with her family in Canada. She was now working in London as Secretary to the Froebel Society. Formed in 1874, it was a foundation which validated examinations and set standards for teaching training courses at pre-school level in the United Kingdom. She was, in her own way, as courageous as her future husband. Earlier in the war she had crossed France by train, then travelled by ship to Alexandria to bring home to England her sister's newly born baby, a feat she accomplished successfully and entirely alone.

By 1917 Henry Morshead had become a Major as well as a recipient of the Distinguished Service Order (DSO), awarded for exceptional service on the western front the previous year. He was transferred to the 33rd Division near Ypres, but in the ever-changing circumstances of war was posted on almost immediately to the 46th Division with the rank of acting Lieutenant Colonel. Henry's war began to draw to a close, when he took a bullet wound to the thigh. He returned to the front, but his war drew fully to its close shortly after his return, due to a severe shrapnel wound which nearly killed him. Four years of battle on the western front, having been twice wounded, ended safely for him. Yet some of his friends were less fortunate, including two of the four survey officers who were on the Tsangpo expedition with him. Morshead returned to India in 1919 and Evie followed him several months later. In October 1920 they settled in Dehra Dun. The house, with expansive views towards the Himalayas, had unsurprisingly been called 'Mountain View', an apposite name as events panned out.

The conquest of Mount Everest had long been in the sights of mountaineers, adventurers, explorers and romantics alike. The difficulties were many and obvious. At over 29,000 feet it was the tallest, most forbidding mountain in the world; oxygen at this altitude was thin and the mountain lay on the border between Tibet and Nepal. Diplomatic permissions to cross these countries and use them as access points to the mountain were hard to obtain and the logistical effort required to sustain a substantial expedition was enormous. British planning for a reconnaissance expedition to the mountain began in 1920 and Tibetan consent was granted in January 1921. The team was to be led by Lieutenant Colonel Charles Howard-Bury and two of the four high climbers selected were Guy Bullock and George Mallory. Henry Morshead, his superb skills as a surveyor having been proven years before on the Tsangpo expedition, was invited to join the team as head of the survey section.

The expedition was to be mounted from Darjeeling, which for the Morsheads entailed a family move from one side of India to the other. It was a tricky move for Evie in particular as she now had a four-month-old son. They spent the first few months living out of suitcases while staying at the Bellevue Hotel in town. Plans for the expedition went relatively smoothly and on 12 May, the day before they set off for Everest, the Governor of Bengal, Lord Ronaldshay, held a send-off dinner party for Howard-Bury and the team. They entered Tibet through Sikkim, reaching Shekar Dzong on 17 June, and then

1921 Everest Expedition team
Back row: Sandy Woolaston, Charles Howard-Bury, Alexander Heron, Harold Raeburn
Front row: George Mallory, Oliver Wheeler, Guy Bullock, Henry Morshead

George Mallory and his beloved wife Ruth, 1916

on to Tingri Maidan, a small trading post fifty miles northwest of Mount Everest, their supply base, which they reached on 19 June. As was necessary on this sort of expedition, they covered huge distances on foot. As a leader in 'The Times' put it: '...*the distance was the same as if they had marched from Hastings to Birmingham via Aldeburgh in Suffolk*'. The three Alpine climbers, Mallory, Bullock and Wheeler reached the North Col of Everest to within 6,000 feet of the summit. The object of the expedition was to carry out reconnaisance for an assault on the summit and this they achieved. Morshead wrote in a letter to his friend Jack Hazard, his former second in command on the Somme: '...*we missed the top of the old mountain by 6,000 feet, but have got the whole country pretty well reconnoitred and surveyed so that the next party to come along will know what they are up against.*'

One would presume that Evie hoped a for return to normality, but it was not to materialise as quickly as she might have wished. Further Everest plans were underway so the family left their temporary hotel accommodation and moved into a house called Chevremont. The Royal Geographical Society and the Alpine Club, the organisers of expeditions to Everest, quickly put together another expedition in 1922. This time the aim was not to carry out further reconnaissance, but to climb the mountain. The expedition leader was a tough Gurkha Officer, Brigadier Charles Bruce, and the team was to include Mallory, the established climber and Morshead. However, as Morshead was not a professionally trained climber, it is surprising that he was picked as a member of the team to climb to the top. Before leaving for Everest, George Mallory came to spend a week with the Morsheads and towards the end of March, they set off.

So very, very near – yet so far. There were three attempts on the summit. Morshead reached 25,000 feet before succumbing to frostbite. George Finch and Geoffrey Bruce reached 27,200 feet, only 1,832 feet short of the summit before frostbite, exhaustion and screaming Tibetan winds forced them back down the mountain. Mallory, Somerville and Finch made the third and final attempt on the summit only to fall just short. The weather had been extremely hard; several members of the team lost one or more digits to frostbite. Morshead was particularly hard hit losing a toe and three fingertips, yet although damaged he applied to the Alpine Club to take part in the already planned 1924 expedition. Given the need for full fitness on the mountain, the Club declined his services as a climber, but requested his involvement as transport and base camp officer, a task he was keen to undertake. However, the Survey of India, wanted him to return to the job. As we know, the 1924 Expedition ended in tragedy. The heroic men, Mallory and Irvine perished on the mountain while attempting to reach the summit. Whether they died before or after achieving their goal continues to remain a subject of debate.

Upperfold, East Ridge, May 1930

Upperfold, a recent photograph

As preparations for the 1924 Everest Expedition gathered pace, Morshead found his non-involvement difficult to stomach. As if it were a form of participation by proxy, he launched into a round of lectures to schools, institutes, regiments and maharajas about Everest, based upon the two expeditions in which he had taken part. His lectures were well received, the entrance fees charged went equally towards forthcoming Everest expedition expenses and to the YWCA. Nevertheless, he felt that he was not doing anything fundamentally useful; his job was routine and his busy social life simply bored him.

Henry was due some leave, so the following year the family sailed to England on the *SS Aquileia*, taking up temporary accommodation in Guildford. Through his close association with the Royal Geographical Society, Henry learned of the planned Cambridge University expedition to Edge Island, Spitzbergen, and was instantly interested. The expedition was to be led by the dashing twenty-year-old Gino Watkins, an early member of the Cambridge University Air Squadron, budding explorer and later yet another brilliant young man to die whilst so doing – in his case by drowning off Greenland. The Edge Island expedition was not a major expedition, but was useful nevertheless. Henry carried out some mapping in the north-west of the island to help disprove the theory that the interior of the island was an icecap. In fact, it was a large valley heavily populated by reindeer and surrounded by an ice ring. This expedition – Gino's first, was to be Henry's last.

After taking seven months leave in England Henry and his family moved to Bangalore, where he was to take up a post in the Southern Circle Office of the Survey of India. In 1928 and back in India, Morshead was promoted to Lieutenant Colonel and looked forward to several more years living in Dehra Dun. However, in early 1929 he received a posting order to Maymyo to take over the job of Director, Burma Circle of the Survey of India. He and four of his children moved to Maymyo in April, without his wife Evie, who remained behind in India for a short while in order to have their fifth child. They travelled via Calcutta, Rangoon and Mandalay arriving a couple of weeks later in Maymyo and moved into 'Upperfold', a comfortable, yet rambling house which stood in a compound of some three acres on the East Ridge, a mile or so from the centre of town and from the Survey of India offices. Morshead was forty-seven years old when he and his family went to live in Maymyo, but as we have discovered, during that time he had achieved more than most might achieve in several lifetimes. After a few weeks Evie arrived with their new child and so for the first time in their married lives the Morsheads found themselves in the happy position of being able to enjoy the rare reality of the entire family being under the same roof, secure in their home in Maymyo.

In simple terms, it was Morshead's job to supervise the mapping of Burma; it was an almost endless task. Much work had been carried out in the previous forty-five years of the British occupation. So whilst much new work on un-surveyed areas was required, a great deal of time was devoted to correcting and revising existing maps. He was assisted by two other Survey officers, Major Kenneth Mason and Captain George Heaney, who became the Surveyor General of India. By a dreadful irony the maps which the team produced were later used extensively by the Japanese when they invaded Burma. The Japanese cartographers who adapted the maps for their own army's use were seemingly possessed with a ghoulish, almost surreal, but perhaps not entirely faux sense of professional etiquette, acknowledging the work of the Survey of India at the foot of their maps.

The family adored Maymyo and Morshead enjoyed his work there. Whilst the social life in India had been frenetic, social life in Maymyo was just right for the Morsheads. There was sufficient time to be sociable and enjoy the company of friends, and time to spend with the children, a balance which Henry and Evie seemed to love.

They both cherished the simple life and being part of Maymyo where they felt settled and happy. Henry took up polo again and the children enjoyed endless rides through the miles of bridleways created by the forestry department. Henry tried to learn Burmese, a notoriously difficult language to master, but with mixed results.

In 1931 after almost three years of work satisfaction and domestic happiness, the fateful day arrived. The time had come for Evie to take the children back to England and put the eldest boys through boarding school. Henry arranged for his sister Ruth to come out to Maymyo and stay with him to help out with household duties and he wrote to Evie regularly while she was away in England. His letters contained detailed accounts of his work, of the social life on the station and the many small domestic issues concerning the house, all of which added up to a happy man, a happy marriage and shared plans for the future. Maymyo, for the Morsheads had been a great success. Now in his third year as Director, Henry was happily looking forward to the fourth year and also to the return of his wife, to whom he wrote in May with detailed suggestions of how and when she should come home to Maymyo. He advised that she should book her passage on the Anchor Line's *SS Tuscania* in October. This unposted letter was written one hour before his death on 17 May and sadly, Evie continued to receive his earlier letters for up to three weeks after she already knew he was dead.

There was much speculation as to how Henry had died and who had killed him. *The Malayan Tribune* reported on 19 May 1931 that his body had been found on a jungle track four miles from Maymyo and that he had severe wounds to the chest and left shoulder. The report suggested that his death might have been as a result of a 'tribal attack'. *The Straits Times* reported the same on 18 May as did *The Singapore Free Press* on 19 May. Days earlier on 16 June *The Singapore Free Press* reported that an ex-Gurkha employee of Henry's had been arrested after admitting that a gun he was carrying had discharged following an altercation with Henry over an issue at work. On 24 June *The Straits Times* printed another, but more detailed story reporting a similar situation. Some locals suggested that the killer may have been part of a gang of Burmese rebels known to be roaming in the area. Henry Morshead's son later suggested in his biography of his father that some thought the murder might have been due to a rumoured relationship between Morshead's sister Ruth and local businessman Syed Ali, but this was later largely discounted in the book. The killer was never found, the case was closed and Henry Morshead, spared at least the misery of seeing two of his four sons killed in action in the Second World War, was buried at the churchyard in Maymyo. His widow never remarried.

'Maymyo will have a botanic garden that will rank with Buitenzorg and Peredinya as an object of pilgrimage. Indeed I think it may even be lovelier. I have no doubt that Maymyo Botanic Garden will be a paradise.'

Reginald Farrer, Plantsman

The Gardener

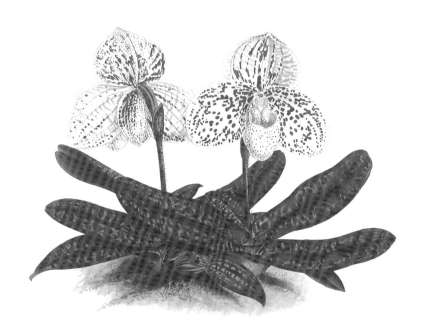

THE GARDENER

Charlotte Wheeler Cuffe

It's a beautiful world! And this is a very beautiful bit of it' wrote Charlotte Wheeler Cuffe to her mother in 1897, three years after she went to live in Burma with her husband Otway. In this book Charlotte features as 'The Gardener', but in truth she could have been included as 'The Artist', for her hundred or so botanical illustrations. Her artwork was as beautiful and professionally executed as was her design of the Botanic Gardens in Maymyo, which she largely if not solely created and which is the major legacy of this highly gifted woman. She was able to combine her wonderful artistic skills, her success as an enthusiastic and successful amateur botanist, and her family role as a loving, supportive and indispensable wife. An extraordinary woman.

Charlotte Isabel Williams was born on 24 May 1867 in Wimbledon, now a suburb of London, but historically in the County of Surrey. Her father William was a prominent solicitor and one-time President of the Law Society and her mother Rose was of Anglo-Irish blood, the daughter of Sir Hercules Langrishe of Knocktopher, County Kilkenny. Charlotte spent most of her childhood in Parkside House, the family home in Wimbledon, but she also spent time at 'Upperfold' the family's country house near Midhurst, in the heart of rural Sussex. Her aunt, Charlotte Langrishe lived at 'Fir Grove' near Thomastown in County Kilkenny, a house that Charlotte and her sister Rosabel visited frequently, and where they developed an enduring love for Ireland.

As far as can be ascertained, Charlotte's childhood was one which would have been considered to be conventional and commensurate with her upper middle-class upbringing. She was endearingly known to the family by the pet name of 'Shadow', due to an early childhood illness which rendered her of pale complexion. Educated at home by a governess until she was eighteen, she then spent the next twelve years enjoying family life, travelling, painting and visiting friends. One of her earliest surviving watercolours dates from a visit to Ireland in 1885, and notes on the reverse of another painting are signed 'W.F. Calderon', suggesting that she attended the Summer School for artists of all abilities that William Calderon conducted at his home during the time he lived in Midhurst. Thus, the inspiration Charlotte gleaned from one of England's most accomplished animal painters was put to spectacular use during her Burma years.

In 1897 Charlotte became engaged to Otway Wheeler Cuffe, whilst he was home on leave from Burma. They had been friends since childhood. Although he was born in Hampshire, Otway's roots were also Anglo-Irish, having grown up at 'Woodlands', his parents' home near Waterford. After school he trained at the Royal Indian Engineering College in Egham, Surrey, prior to joining the Public Works Department (PWD) in Burma around 1890. The PWD had been created by the colonial administration in India and charged by the administration with taking over various non-military engineering tasks previously carried out by the Sappers and Miners Regiments of the three Indian Presidencies. Not considered to be one of the more exotic branches of the state, its function was vital. The movement of goods and people by road or rail transport, defence works, Government and administration in general, even economic growth, would all have proved impossible without the PWD dealing with the unglamorous, but crucial work of building and maintaining roads, bridges, railways, irrigation ditches and waterways and various state buildings ranging from small, local police posts to grand government buildings.

The marriage took place within weeks, because Otway was due to return to Burma in the middle of the year and Charlotte absolutely refused to be left behind. Then two weeks later the couple sailed from Liverpool on Bibby Line's *SS Staffordshire* bound for Rangoon. It was a popular route to the Far East; Bibby, P&O and Paddy Henderson ships frequently sailed past one another as they plied the ocean back and forth to their destinations. The twenty-eight day journey took them through the Bay of Biscay, across the Mediterranean, through the Suez Canal, the Red Sea and out into the Indian Ocean, then on to Colombo, Ceylon and the final leg over the Bay of Bengal to Burma. During the voyage, Charlotte read a borrowed copy of George Bird's

Wanderings in Burma in order to familiarise herself with her new home. It is a beautifully written, well-illustrated guide to Burma, including its cities and shrines.

Four weeks after it left England the *SS Staffordshire* steamed into Rangoon. The Cuffes stayed in the city for only a week before travelling up-country by train to Prome, then onwards by IFC steamer to Thayetmyo, the place to which Otway Cuffe had been posted to take up the position of PWD executive engineer. Thayetmyo or 'Mango Town' is an ancient town founded in 1306 by Min Shin Saw, son of Kyaw Zwa, the last King of Pagan. It lies on the Irrawaddy river 200 miles north of Rangoon and was, in the Cuffe's day, a quiet little town with a population of around 17,500. The cantonment where Charlotte would have lived was on high, undulating ground close to the river, not far from the small fort which housed the arsenal.

As in most small settlements there was a church, a library and a club which provided the occasional distraction, but for a couple increasingly keen to paint and go on tour, it was little more than that – a distraction. Otway toured his district extensively and although unusual for the time, he often took Charlotte. Unfortunately, only a few of her earlier paintings have survived, but in 1906, on one of the early tours with her husband, she painted the *Dendrobium* species of orchid, which she had seen on the Arakan mountains which lay between the Irrawaddy and the Bay of Bengal.

The Cuffes spent two years in Thayetmyo then took long leave in Ireland, later returning to Burma to a new posting in the town of Toungoo, east of Thayetmyo on the Sittang river. However, they had little time to settle in. The demands of the Service dictated the pace and nature of their lives, as it affected the lives of all Government servants and no sooner had they begun to find their feet in Toungoo, than Otway received another posting order, this time to Mandalay.

In letters to her mother Charlotte made no secret of her dislike of Toungoo, or more particularly, some of the people with whom she had to associate in the town. But she loved the area now under Otway's supervision, which included the ruby mining area of Mogok where she found many beautiful orchids. Furthermore, she enjoyed life in Mandalay where she helped local church committees and similar institutions, but, importantly, she advised and became directly involved in the redesign of the gardens in Fort Dufferin.

Mandalay lies on the central plain on the east bank of the Irrawaddy river. It is a hot, humid city, particularly from March to October when temperatures can reach forty-five degrees centigrade. For the fortunate few, Maymyo, forty miles to the east and situated at 3,500 feet, provided an easy-to-reach sanctuary from the heat. It was a place the Cuffes sought out and enjoyed, visiting often, staying with friends and making new contacts who would serve them well in the coming years.

Another posting order arrived for Otway, this time he was instructed to go to Meiktila, a small garrison town sixty miles south of Mandalay, built on the eastern side of a six mile long lake. Charlotte's sketch map of Meiktila shows her accomplished cartographic skills and her keen eye for detail and accuracy borne out of her experience as a botanical artist. She continued to accompany Otway on his travels, sometimes hundreds of miles in hot and arduous conditions. However, in letters home she revealed that such tours were not a duty but a pleasure, allowing her to discover and then paint beautiful plants, particularly orchids. It was on some of these tours from Meiktila that she appears to have realised her love for the Shan hills and she writes fulsomely of a trip to the hill station of Kalaw, past *'cosy villages…cheery Shans…and jolly fat children'* before returning to Meiktila via the arduous Natteik Pass. Charlotte and Otway also visited Pagan where the Public Works Department were responsible for the maintenance of some of the 2,000 ancient stupas or pagodas which were at the spiritual heart of this former Kingdom. They had thrived for centuries before succumbing to relentless pressure from the Mongols on the northern fringes of its empire.

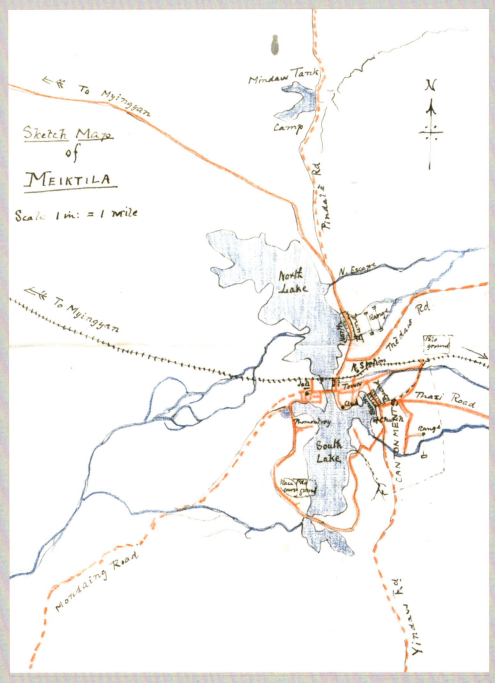
Charlotte's sketch map of Meiktila

One of Charlotte's sketch plans for the Maymyo Botanic Gardens

Later in the year Otway received news of his father's death, so he took compassionate leave and returned to Ireland to organise his father's affairs. Charlotte, who had been feeling unwell, consulted a doctor in Dublin who prescribed an operation which, tragically, would mean that she would be unable to have children. The operation was a success and she remained in the UK for several months to recover whilst Otway returned to his job in Burma. Shortly after Charlotte returned to Meiktila yet another posting order arrived and they found themselves heading off to Rangoon for a second time. They arrived in Kokine, a suburb of Rangoon, where they had lived during their first Rangoon posting. Otway was to be the Superintending Engineer in the capital, with responsibility for all of the main buildings, hospitals and infrastructure works – a satisfying and important post, although Charlotte was disappointed to leave behind the magnificent garden which she had created in Meiktila.

It was in the Spring of 1911 while living in Mandalay that Charlotte received an invitation, the result of which placed her amongst the top echelon of botanists who discover new or hitherto unknown plants to Western eyes. Winifred Macnabb, wife of a Deputy Commissioner, planned to spend part of the hot weather in a cool climate 10,000 feet up Mount Victoria on the edge of the Chin hills in western Burma. She invited Charlotte to join her and despite some misgivings about leaving Otway alone, she was overjoyed. She knew that she would see some beautiful orchids and other plants in the hills. The two ladies repeated the trip in 1912, starting from the small military outpost of Kampetlet on the edge of the Chin hills. On her return she sent several orchid specimens to Sir Frederick Moore, Director of the Royal Botanic Gardens at Glasnevin near Dublin, at least three of which were hitherto unknown to Western botanists; *Anemone obtusiloba*, which became known as Shadow's Buttercup, the yellow *Rhododendron burmanicum* and her 'chief find' and the plant which was to be named after her, the white *Rhododendron cuffeeanum*. She found this plant at around 8,000 feet and it was, she wrote, *'a sweet scented, snow white rhododendron which grows like an orchid on other trees, never on the ground. I have got a lot of plants of it and will try to send some home. It does not seem to grow naturally below 7,000 ft …it is very beautiful.'*

On her return from her first trip to Mount Victoria in 1911, Charlotte was commissioned to illustrate a children's book entitled *The Burma Alphabet*. Each letter of the alphabet was to be accompanied by an illustration by Charlotte. The book was published in English and Burmese and was priced at five rupees per copy, the funds raised going towards the Queen Alexandra's Children's Hospital which was under construction in Mandalay. The project was a great success; the book sold well and raised a substantial sum of money for the hospital. It was an exquisite production, a delight of beautiful art and charming couplets – now a rare collectors' item. It was her only published book.

Otway Wheeler Cuffe received the final posting order of his career in 1913. The destination was Maymyo in the Shan hills. At first, Charlotte did not take to Maymyo; too many moves perhaps, too many gardens left behind for others to enjoy or sometimes ignore. But her eternal optimism and sunny disposition came quickly to the fore and not long after her arrival she wrote to her mother saying of Maymyo *'this is the best Circle in Burma from every point of view'*. They changed the name of their house, 'Bamboo Lodge' (which Charlotte regarded as banal) to 'Upperfold', one of her happy childhood homes. She threw herself into her new garden project at home, and due to her energy and an ideal climate, within two years the garden was alive with colour – orchids and the driveway full of roses, violets and gladioli. The richness and exuberance of her garden provided them both with succour during the war when friends and family members lost their lives, many of them on the Western Front including Otway's cousin Charlie. He would have inherited the house at Leyrath in Ireland and the baronetcy of his father Sir Charles Wheeler Cuffe. After Sir Charles died in 1915 the baronetcy then passed to Otway who became Sir Otway and Charlotte, Lady Charlotte. Charlotte kept busy with the church, the choir, the hospital and a choral

Rhododendron cuffeanum

Rhododendron burmanicum

society and also sat on the committee of six charged with the restoration of the gardens at the Royal Palace in Mandalay. However, it is the Botanic Gardens in Maymyo with which her name will be forever associated; for she was the driving force behind the project. Her energy and expert eye created the gardens which are still alive and cherished to this day.

Evidence as to when the Botanic Gardens in Maymyo were actually begun conflicts a little, but 1914 seems to be the year when the idea of creating a garden was discussed and formalised. Alec Rodger, President of the Indian Forestry Institute, Gilbert (Bertie) Rogers, Chief Conservator of Forests and Mandalay and Maymyo-based lawyer Rodway Swinhoe, formed the group which gave life to the idea.

The Burma Forestry Service was to administer the gardens and the project was given the backing of the Lieutenant Governor, Sir Spencer Harcourt Butler. It is likely that the gardens would have been completed more quickly had not the war intervened, claiming the time of some and the lives of others. Rodger persuaded the Government to buy thirty acres on which to create the gardens, but he was soon to be wearing a second 'hat' as Deputy Controller of Munitions, so the time he could devote to garden development became limited. To her delight in October 1917, Charlotte was asked by Gilbert Rogers and the Government's chief revenue officer William Keith to assume the role of Clerk of Works. To Sir Frederick Moore she wrote: *'I am to be turned loose with a gang of labourers to work my wicked will. I am fearfully excited over it all and dream of masses of lovely plants and rock and water garden and all sorts of delectable plans and schemes.'*

Charlotte gave the job her utmost. She was on site before seven-thirty in the morning on most days and worked throughout the day. The emphasis was placed on using indigenous plants, not only from the Shan hills, but from all over Burma. However, she could not resist adding a *'parcel of seeds and roots from the Mesopotamia-Persia frontier'* sent to her by a friend, as well as some *'cyclamen from Jerusalem'* which she found just too exciting to ignore. She was hugely reliant on her right-hand-man, Maung Khin, a Burmese of firm grip and great skill; a keen gardener and botanist who could also survey, level and build. They both relied on the Burmese workers. She was particularly impressed by their knowledge of plants, which, from time to time, they would bring in from the jungle for her. It was the experience of working with the knowledgeable, hardworking and fully committed Burmese which made her determined that the gardens should be accessible to everyone. Therefore, labels were written in English, anglicised Burmese and in Burmese script as well.

Charlotte was confident enough to ask anyone and everyone if she required help. At one point, Queen Victoria's Own Sappers and Miners were co-opted out of Mandalay to assist with some of the specialist groundworks. John List, a District Officer of her acquaintance was badgered into arranging for a sun dial to be carved by skilled stonemasons in Mandalay. What began just a few years earlier as thirty acres, by November 1918 had grown to one hundred and fifty acres. Friends and acquaintances gathered plants for her from Lashio, the Panwa Pass, Hpimaw and the Karind Valley, in addition to those provided from Glasnevin and those which Charlotte collected herself from the hills in and around Maymyo.

In 1919 the Wheeler Cuffes took their first home leave since the beginning of the war, and visited the Botanic Gardens in Peredinya, Ceylon on the way back to England. They visited Kew Gardens in London and Glasnevin in Dublin so that Charlotte could return to Maymyo bursting with excitement and full of new ideas. However, excitement turned to sadness upon realising that they had less than eighteen months left in Burma before Otway would be forced into age-related compulsory retirement. Her garden was a complete triumph. The brilliant, Balliol educated, harshly critical plantsman Reginald Farrer who tragically died in northern Burma the following year, wrote of Charlotte's garden: *'Maymyo will have a botanic garden that will rank with Buitenzorg (Dutch East Indies) and Peredinya (Ceylon) as an object of pilgrimage.*

Charlotte's sketch of a view of the Mamyo Gardens landscape, 1921

Indeed I think it may even be lovelier… I have no doubt that Maymyo Botanic Garden will be a paradise.' Charlotte, wrote to Sir Frederick Moore early in 1921, saying: *'We are leaving Burma for good this month and it is a great wrench but 'anno domini' is a thing one cannot contend against and my husband must retire under the age limit'.* Compulsory retirement at such a young age for employees from all branches of Government service, whether from the Army, Indian Civil Service, Foreign Office and other Civil Service branches, adversely affected many men ahead of their time; they simply faded and declined. Charlotte and Otway left their *'dear, beautiful laughing Burma'* and retired to Leyrath, near Kilkenny in Ireland. They loved Leyrath and were happy there, but for both, Burma, particularly Maymyo and Charlotte's beautiful gardens, had been their glory, the very best days of their lives. The Anglo-Irish writer, Elizabeth Bowen wrote that when looking back to the joyous years of her youth, days of her now so long gone way of life impossible to recreate, she saw a past which had become *'like sunshine elsewhere or firelight in an empty room.'* It must have been like that for Charlotte on losing Otway when he died in 1934. He was not only her husband but her living link with Burma. She outlived him by thirty-three years and died in 1967, just weeks before her 100th birthday.

Blue buttercup – Anemone obtusiloba

Rhododendron htawgaw

Dendrobium

Dendrobium fimbriatum

Dendrobium gratiosissimum

Pecteilis susanner

THE GARDENER

Rose from Kutkai

Dendrobium thyrsiflorum

Charlotte Wheeler Cuffe's Burma Alphabet *(front cover), published in Mandalay, 1913*

THE GARDENER

Page from Charlotte Wheeler Cuffe's Burma Alphabet *published in 1913*

'When Burma obtained self-government
he was the obvious choice as Commander-in-Chief,
and was duly selected. His record was,
therefore, outstanding, rising as he did from the ranks
by merit-promotion to
become a Commander-in-Chief.'

Major General David Tennant 'Punch' Cowan

The Soldier

Smith Dun handed over his office and his job to his second in command and successor on 1 February 1949, said goodbye to his friends, colleagues and staff, returned home to pack his bags, said a further goodbye to Rangoon then within days, moved north with his family, eventually settling in Maymyo. Not a natural choice of home perhaps for a Karen who might ordinarily have been expected to retire to Karen state in the east of the country, but Smith Dun knew the Shan hills. He had served there for a brief while during the Second World War and felt an affinity with the place. He believed that if he could be content anywhere it would be there, away from the politics of Rangoon. To him the Shan hills were an arcadia where ethnic strife, beginning to trouble the rest of Burma, barely existed. One might think of it as a happy retirement haven for an 'ordinary' retired soldier – bucolic bliss under a Shan hills heaven until the day when anno domini catches up and the remaining friends muster slowly and voice their goodbyes too. But this was no ordinary soldier, this was Lieutenant General Smith Dun MC, winner of the Sword of Honour (for best officer cadet) at the Indian Military Academy in Dehra Dun. He was the first Burmese officer to hold the King's Commission in the 1st Punjab regiment. He was a veteran of operations against the Pathans on the north-west frontier in the 1930s and a veteran of the war against the Japanese in Burma, for which he was awarded the Military Cross for gallantry in the face of the enemy. He was twice mentioned in despatches. He rose to become the first Commander-in-Chief of the post-independence Burmese Army in the rank of Lieutenant General. He was no 'ordinary' soldier.

We have heard little of Smith Dun. In the modern Burma he has been airbrushed from post-independence history, the reasons for which will become evident as his story unfolds, but there was something special about him. In the foreword to Smith Dun's memoirs, General David (Punch) Cowan, commander of the 17th Indian Division with which Smith Dun served during the war, a man not known for hyperbole, said of him: *'when Burma obtained self-government he was the obvious choice as Commander-in-Chief, and was duly selected. His record was, therefore, outstanding, rising as he did from the ranks by merit-promotion to become a Commander-in Chief.'* Cowan had it absolutely right – merit was the reason for this man's success.

Po Yay, later Smith Dun, was born to farming parents in Bassein in Burma's Irrawaddy Province on 11 November 1906. He was educated locally at first, then later at the American Baptist Mission School in Bassein, but was not a particularly academic child. However, what he lacked in brainpower, he made up for in fitness, stamina, agility and sheer guts. *'There is nothing very much in this',* he once said to a general during the war, whilst pointing to his own head. From his earliest days he wanted to become a soldier. As a boy he was impressed by the confidence and swagger of the Karen recruiting sergeants of the Burma Rifles who often toured his local area looking for 'likely lads'. He listened for hours to his brother recalling his adventures during the First World War, from which he returned as a *naik* or corporal. One day, during his mid-teens, the allure of uniform proved too much for Po Yay, so he left school and headed for the nearest Burma Rifles unit where he volunteered. He was just sixteen years old and barely touched five feet two inches, but his enthusiasm and strong build won over the recruiters; he was enlisted and began his training. However, Po Yay's family were opposed to this move, thinking him much too young to join the army. Three months into his training his father tracked him down and appealed to the Commanding Officer. As a result Po Yay found himself back at school for another year. But he was not deterred and as soon as he finished his schooling he re-enlisted with the Burma Rifles. He signed on in November 1924 and was sent to complete his training with the battalion in Maymyo. This was his first taste of the Shan hills.

So, you may ask why was he called Smith Dun and not Po Yay? Just before he left Bassein he visited the cinema with his close friend Hanson Kya Doe to watch a film in which the great hulking hero was called Smith. It was customary

THE SOLDIER

Lieutenant General Smith Dun

Above: 17th Indian Division badge
Above left: Burma Rifles badge
Centre: 1st Punjab Regiment badge

Smith Dun's military medals (left to right)

1. Military Cross
2. India General Service Medal 1908-1935 with Burma clasp
3. General Service Medal 1936-1937 with North-West Frontier clasp
4. 1939-1945 Star Campaign Medal
5. Burma Star Campaign Medal
6. Defence Medal 1939-1945
7. Victory Medal 1945 with Mentioned in Despatches leaf

in those days for some Karen to adopt western names, so Po Yay chose the name Smith after his screen idol. Later he added his father's surname Dun to conform with Army protocol. Smith and Hanson trained together in the same company, and at the successful conclusion of their basic training they were both posted to the 2nd battalion of the regiment stationed in Taiping, a quiet, pretty town in the State of Perak in Malaya.

Smith and Hanson prospered well in the Regiment, both gaining a stripe per year, so after three years each was a *havildar* or sergeant. More promotions and opportunities followed rapidly. Both were by now considered worthy and capable of holding commissions. Hanson was awarded a place at the Royal Military College, Sandhurst, from where he would graduate with the King's Commission. Smith Dun was promoted to *jemadar* or lieutenant in the regiment as the education officer, largely on account of his linguistic skills; he spoke three languages fluently.

The break which really set his career on the path to success came as Indian politicians were lobbying for a process of Indianisation in the officer ranks of the army. To foster this legitimate desire, the army created the Indian Military Academy (IMA) at Dehra Dun in 1932. Its Commandant was the highly decorated 4th Gurkha Brigadier Lionel Peter Collins, a man renowned for getting things done.

Lieutenant-Colonel Sandernam, the Commandant of the Burma Rifles, believed that Smith was made of the right stuff for the new IMA, so he sent him to Kitchener College in Nowgong to study for his Army Special Certificate. Smith Dun passed the examination with flying colours. He was now set for Dehra Dun where he arrived in October 1932 to attend the very first course among a group of forty officer cadets. His Company Commander was Major David Tennant Cowan MC of the 6th Gurkha Rifles, the same officer who, only a few years later, in the rank of Major-General, was commanding the 17th Indian Division, resisting the invading Japanese.

Smith Dun was in esteemed company at the IMA. Several of his fellow officer cadets had glittering careers, rising to senior ranks in either the Indian, Burmese or Pakistan armies. One officer, Sam Manekshaw, rose to the rank of Field-Marshal and his reputation in the Indian Army and his standing in India became huge.

One cannot overstate the degree to which Smith Dun excelled on his officer training course at Dehra Dun, given the quality of many of his fellow officer cadets. Suffice to say that officer training colleges run by the British, award the highly prized Sword of Honour to the best student at the end of each course on commissioning. In 1924 Smith Dun won the very first Sword of Honour awarded by the new IMA at Dehra Dun, a magnificent achievement. In his speech to the officer cadets at the inauguration of the IMA, Field-Marshal Sir Philip Chetwode said: *'The safety, honour and welfare of your country come first, always and every time. The honour, welfare and comfort of the men you command come next. Your own ease, comfort and safety come last, always and every time.'*

This statement was inscribed on the oak panelling in the hall of the IMA and remains there to this day. Smith Dun was so inspired by these words that he positioned them prominently in his autobiography. It is clear from a study of the record of this honourable officer, that he very much lived by them. He was commissioned 2nd Lieutenant into the 1st Punjabis, an Indian Army Infantry Regiment with a great reputation and a long history. Its roots can be traced back to 1759, when its antecedents were part of the East India Company's Madras Army. By a happy coincidence his old friend Hanson Kya Doe, recently commissioned from RMC Sandhurst, also joined the same regiment. However, Smith Dun was required to spend a year with a British regiment before joining his own Indian regiment. This rule applied to all officers joining the Indian Army irrespective of their nationality – British, Indian or Burmese. He was seconded to the King's Own Yorkshire Light Infantry in Agra. Dun writes briefly but fondly of this year of secondment, yet one can sense his eagerness for time to pass so that he could at last join his own regiment. The 2nd Battalion of the 1st Punjabis was stationed at Razmak on the northwest frontier. Almost immediately Smith Dun found himself taking part in operations against the Fakir of Ipi who was fighting, as the Pathans usually were, against the British Raj. This was serious soldiering; the Pathans were hardy, courageous, and they knew their ground. They were excellent marksmen and they bordered on the fanatical. Tactical errors by the British were never overlooked or forgiven by the Pathans, as Kipling pointed out in his poem *'Arithmetic on the Frontier'* as he recounts the death of a young officer:

'A scrimmage in a border station,
A canter down some dark defile,
Two thousand pounds of education
Drops to a ten-rupee jezail.'

Smith Dun survived the frontier unscathed, as did his friend Hanson, and at the end of the tour the battalion was posted to the city of Multan in the Punjab and assigned to internal security duties. By 1939 Burma had been detached from India for two years via the Separation Act; it was no longer merely a 'province'. The administration in Burma, Burmese politicians in particular, were keen to bring their 'own' back to work developing Burma's domestic institutions and state. Here was an opportunity for Smith Dun to assist in his own country's development, and it was one that he relished. Therefore, he applied to join the Burma Military Police (BMP). It would seem from his notes that his application was strongly supported by his commanding officer in the 1st Punjabis; nor would his application have been hindered by the presence of a cousin in the Legislative Council in Rangoon. His application to join the BMP was accepted and he returned home with a light heart, full of optimism and

General Sam Manekshaw inspecting the Irish Guards on an official visit to the UK

THE SOLDIER

Soldiers of the 4th Gurkha Rifles involved in a rear-guard action. Painting by Alfred Crowdy-Lovett (1862-1919)

confidence. From the outset he loved the job. It involved very little office work and many tours and inspections of BMP outposts around the country. He described the job as 'rosy'. But it was not rosy for long. In late 1941, the Japanese Army, having already laid waste to south China, occupied Siam and attacked Hong Kong, Malaya and the Dutch East Indies. Pearl Harbour in Honolulu was also bombed in pursuit of Japan's own form of 'lebensraum'. Crucially, they sought the commodities which were not available to them within their own territories. The Far East was in flames; now Burma's own bloody and chaotic descent into war began. On 23 December 1941 the Japanese bombed Rangoon causing carnage. According to sources 2,000 died and catastrophic damage was caused. By radio that evening the Japanese warned that they would repeat their attack on Christmas Day and true to their word, they did so with equal ferocity. In spite of the chaos, Dun removed his family from Rangoon into the countryside and did not see them again until the final months of the war.

In January 1942 the military situation deteriorated rapidly. Despite assurances from the administration that Rangoon would hold out at all costs, it was clear to professional soldiers that the city could not possibly be held. The fall of Rangoon came as a terrible blow, but Smith Dun was unsurprised when the evacuation order was issued on 20 February 1942. Both battalions of the BMP were ordered to withdraw north, only for a counter-order to be given to Dun's battalion to return to Rangoon to deal with a scourge of looting which had begun shortly after the army began to withdraw. On 7 March complete evacuation of the city was ordered, and the serious ordeal for civilians began. Many of the Burmese civilians could melt away to the villages from where they or their families came. However, there were no villages for the Indian, Chinese and British populations of Rangoon to go. They had no choice but to trek north, a journey which resulted in suffering and death along the trail north-west towards India. By late March, both BMP battalions had suffered casualties and desertions, so it was decided to amalgamate them. Dun was ordered to HQ 17th Indian Division to act as the liaison officer between the HQ and the BMP. There he met Divisional Commander, Major General Punch Cowan, his Company Commander from the IMA. This was a fortuitous meeting and a reminder to each of happier times.

As the division withdrew north to Tharrawaddy, the rate of desertion, particularly by the Karen, increased. As a Karen himself, this hit Dun hard; he felt shamed by the desertions. But when he voiced his concerns to the Battalion second-in-command, a Major Jones, he was told not to feel so shamed as the melting away of the Karen was quite understandable, because they could actually see their villages from the main roads. Moreover, they knew that the Burmese Independence Army (BIA), friends of the Japanese, were infiltrating the villages and robbing and killing the inhabitants. Jones' far-sighted view probably resulted in the saving of many Karen lives, for when the army came back down through Burma two years later, it was evident that the Karen deserters had taken on the gangs of *dacoits* thereby saving their villages from destruction. The division continued its withdrawal along the Prome road becoming involved in serious fighting with the Japanese and the BIA at Shwedaung before crossing the Irrawaddy over the Ava bridge. When the bridge was blown, Dun felt for the first time that Burma really was lost to the Japanese. They pressed on north pausing at Pyin-gaing before ultimately passing through the 23rd Indian Division's defence perimeter and arriving, exhausted, at Imphal.

There was little time to rest. Already plans were afoot for the retaking of Burma and the expulsion of the Japanese army. Quickly the division began to reorganise and refit in preparation for the long hard road back down country to Rangoon. General Cowan had other ideas for Dun. He was to be sent to the Staff College in Quetta, a sure sign of his General's confidence in him and a further sign that he was being groomed for senior levels of command. He flew out of Imphal and after a few weeks leave in Calcutta, most of which was spent recovering from malaria, he arrived in Quetta. In his memoirs Dun complained repeatedly about

THE SOLDIER

Soldier of the 3rd Gurkha Rifles engaged in house-to-house fighting in a Burmese village, 1945

his own intellectual abilities, yet he was not intellectually challenged in the least. He received a good report from the staff college and was returned to Cowan's 17th Division, promoted to Major and Chief Liaison Officer between the division and the Burma Intelligence Corps (BIC). Each division had a platoon of BIC, whose jobs included the collation of intelligence about the Japanese gleaned from local Burmese, translations and interpreting, and to being the forward eyes and ears of the division. To this latter end, Dun established a standing patrol in the Chin hills south of Tiddim, in conjunction with Chin irregulars from where they would reconnoitre forward and learn as much as they could from the locals about Japanese dispositions. Quite frequently Dun Force as it was known, established its own highly effective ambushes against the Japanese and scored more than a few kills, using intelligence they themselves had gained. When back in the Imphal perimeter they were repeatedly attacked by the Japanese and losses mounted, some of which Dun felt personally. He described, with deep-felt sadness, the death of a young British Captain and friend, who, although wounded during a raid, continued to attempt to repel the attacking Japanese. When at last he fell to a mortal wound, he uttered the pitiful words *'tell mother'*. As made clear in his memoirs, Dun was also saddened during the retreat by the sight of a child on the roadside attempting to suckle from his dead mother. Dun soldiered through some very grim times and witnessed some terrible events, many of which remained with him for life.

After war-leave in Mhow, India in October 1944 for Dun and his platoon, he was posted back to Burma to join the 7th Indian Division at Tamu, with a company composed largely of Karen soldiers, most of whom were ex-Burma Rifles. No sooner had he re-joined than the Division began to push down the Gangaw valley towards the Irrawaddy. Dun's division secured the crossing over which the 17th Indian Division leapfrogged as they headed south to take Meiktila. The 14th Army was making rapid progress against the now weakened and increasingly demoralised Japanese. Dun noted in his memoirs: *'If our withdrawal in 1942 was swift, our advance in 1945 was just as swift, if not faster …division after division hooking left and right and town after town falling'.* It became like a race, so rapidly did the Japanese collapse. Dun was sent to Henzada north-west of Rangoon to ascertain Japanese strength in the town. He found only Karens and BIA, united only in their hatred of the Japanese. He then pushed on to Bassein, 120 miles west of Rangoon. Although still operating in small pockets in the area, the town had been largely abandoned by the Japanese army, which had by then lost all cohesion. Going to Bassein was important for Dun, not only because of the job he had been given, but because his family were in the area and he had neither seen nor heard of or from them since the 1942 withdrawal. At length he found them safe, but for his youngest child, who had died tragically from a lack of medication early during the occupation.

Major General DT Cowan, 17th Indian Division Burma Campaign 1941-1945, conducting a staff conference

Recalled to Rangoon after the defeat of the Japanese, Dun was promoted to Brigadier and appointed Deputy General Officer Commanding (DGOC) of the Burma Army. In 1947, just months before independence he was promoted again, to Major-General and appointed GOC Burma Army, the first Burmese officer to be appointed thus. He took over at a difficult time. General Aung San, the father of Burmese independence, had been assassinated in July 1947. Ardently nationalistic, Aung San had opposed vehemently the British initiated Frontiers Areas Committee of enquiry, whose job it was to ascertain the extent of support for some form of independence post-war, for the Karen and other tribal states. Smith Dun, a Karen commanding an all-Burma Army, felt compromised from the outset.

Burma gained independence from Great Britain on 4 January 1948 and almost immediately fell into a state of turmoil. In Smith Dun's view, this was caused by those who thought they deserved the lion's share of various post-war spoils, but had failed to get them. By this time he had become a Lieutenant-General and was appointed to be the Supreme Commander of all of Burma's armed forces, surely one of the most rapid series of promotions in modern military history. However, Smith Dun had his hands full. An almost entirely ethnically Burmese communist insurgency was creating fear, chaos and desertions of Burmese from the Army over to the rebels. This caused considerable disquiet in Rangoon as even Burmese politicians and Army officers began to wonder just who they could trust. Dun had the answer: Karens, Chins and Gurkhas and he relied on them hugely. When the Burma Rifles mutinied at Thayetmayo and seized Prome, a battalion of Kachin Rifles was ordered to retake the town which they duly did, with speed and efficiency. By this time it was only hill tribe troops upon whom Smith Dun and the Rangoon-based general staff could rely. Shortly afterwards, what would now be called ethnic cleansing began with attacks on the Karen inhabitants of Ahlone and Thaimang. When news of these attacks reached Karen troops based in Mingaladon they also mutinied and left for home to protect their kith and kin.

The breakdown of law and order was now almost complete. The fighting then spread to Insein near the capital where Karen troops gained the upper hand against Burmese former BIA troops. At this difficult juncture Dun, a Karen, felt he could only remain as GOC with the full and unequivocal support of the politicians and general staff. Unfortunately, support was not clearly and unequivocally forthcoming; therefore he resigned. Early the next morning at about 7am General Dun and his family left their residence in two cars for the airport to fly to Meiktila from where they would travel by road to Kalaw in the Shan hills. As they drove to the airport, two-inch mortars and small arms were fired on the vehicles, both of which took rapid and effective evasive action and sped away. Dun was understandably furious at this attempt on his, and more importantly, his family's lives, but there was little he could do about it. He commandeered an ambulance that was parked by the District Commander's residence and thus disguised, drove to the airport. He and his family flew to Meiktila only to be warned on arrival that he was not to drive on to Kalaw. The risks posed by insurgents and mutineers were deemed to be too great, so they pressed on by road to Maymyo. Maymyo itself was passing back and forth between Burmese troops, Karens and Kachins, so the family moved on to Myitkyina and Dun joined them on 19 May 1949. Later in the year and as things quietened down, the Dun family moved back to the Shan States. He spent the remaining thirty years of his life living in Maymyo and Kalaw, doing a little farming here and remembering there. Never did he attempt to exact any form of revenge on those who had failed to support him when he was GOC. Never did he become involved in politics, nor did he write letters or articles critical of the regime's conduct in 1948; exemplary conduct from a very proper officer.

When Dun resigned as GOC in February 1949 he handed over his job to his second in command, General Ne Win who then succeeded him as GOC. Burma and the world were later to find out just how that was to transpire. General Smith Dun MC was a proud Karen, a loyal Burmese citizen and a good soldier. He died in 1979.

'Her still handsome features were continually enlivened by an expression which made one feel she was amused by something of which she did not entirely approve.'

Norman Lewis, Travel Writer

The Princesses

THE PRINCESSES

It was a particularly brutal, mid-19th century murder at the palace in Mandalay which altered the course of history and changed the lives of the Princesses Teik Tin Ma Lat and her daughter Yadana Nat Mai, the Goddess of the Nine Jewels. The murder took place long before either of the princesses were born, and but for the murder, Ma Lat's father Prince Limbin, would have been regarded as a legitimate and likely heir to the Burmese throne. Had he succeeded, Princess Ma Lat and Princess Yadana Nat Mai would have been daughter and granddaughter respectively of the Burmese king. However, the murder set the whole family on an entirely different path.

King Mindon of the Konbaung dynasty came to power in 1852 after overthrowing his brother King Pagan at the end of the disastrous second Anglo-Burma War, a war which led to the annexation of Lower Burma by the British. History records that Mindon was a popular king; fair, forward thinking and an enlightened moderniser who reorganised and improved the governance and administration of his country. He sent many young Burmese students to Europe to study engineering, commerce and science in order to help with the development of the country. Mindon was most definitively an advocate of social and economic progress; he was on the side of change. His great ally in this programme of modernisation was his brother and heir apparent, the Prince of Kenaung. However, Mindon's sons, the Princes of Myingun and Myinkhondaing were not of the same mould as their father; they looked backwards. They were political revanchists and monarchical absolutists and in a plot to reverse the reforms being enacted by their father and uncle they mounted a coup against the king on 2 August 1866. However, they had given insufficient thought to Mindon's popularity and the coup failed. But during the mêlée and the accompanying extensive slaughter they succeeded in killing their uncle, the prince, beheading him in the grounds of the palace. The murdered prince of Kenaung was Princess Yadana Nat Mai's great grandfather. Several of the prince's sons had also been murdered in the attempted coup, but one son, Maung Kin Kin Gyi, Prince of Limbin, escaped the bloodshed by a whisker and travelled south to Lower Burma to find safety. He took service with the British administration in Lower Burma as the *Myook* or Township Officer of Henzada. He remained in post until the early 1880s when the authorities learned that he was becoming increasingly supportive of resistance to the British presence in Upper Burma, the resistance being led by the late King Mindon's son, King Thibaw. The prince was dismissed from his job and in 1885 he fled to Kengtung, joining a nascent rebellion with the rebel *sawbwas*, a revolt that did not last long. Accepting British suzerainty after the Third Anglo-Burmese War, he was exiled to India with Thibaw and several other princes, not returning to Burma until 1911. Exile did not become incarceration, nor were harsh conditions imposed upon the prince and members of his family. Indeed, they even received modest living expenses from the Government, but nevertheless had become exiles. They had lost their lands and homes in the Shan States, they had left friends and extended family behind and they forfeited the privileged life of Shan aristocrats. Exile is a lonely state and theirs was lengthy. They did not see Burma again for nearly a quarter of a century.

The family had to build a new life as exiles in India and they spent three years in Calcutta before settling in northern India in the city of Allahabad on the junction of the Ganges and Yamuna rivers. The Prince of Limbin had four sons and six daughters by two different wives. One daughter, Princess Teik Tin Ma Lat, was born in Calcutta on 13 October 1894 and was educated at the well-regarded Girl's High School in Allahabad, one of several founded on the English public school model. She was a beautiful child who grew up to be a strikingly attractive young woman. She made many friends and contacts at school and in social circles and as she grew older, she was welcomed into 'smart' society, by courtesy of her royal blood and her extraordinarily good looks. Ma Lat would have been seen as most suitable for marriage, but it was her beauty, vivacity and crucially, eligibility, which led, unwittingly, to yet a further blow to the family on top of their exile.

North of India and sandwiched between Nepal to the west, Tibet to the north and Bhutan to the east, lay the Buddhist Kingdom of Sikkim. It is a Shangri-La of mountains, rivers and an ancient and peaceful way of life under Priest-Kings of the Namgyal family or dynasty. The 1817 Treaty of Titalia established British influence over Sikkimese foreign relations following a convoluted series of events reaching back to the 1815 Anglo-Nepal war, in which the Sikkimese assisted the British, for which the British returned Sikkim land lost to the Nepalese in earlier wars.

The Sikkimese also granted the British the right to establish a sanatorium at the village of Dorje Ling (later Darjeeling). In Sikkimese culture all land belonged to the king, so as far as the Sikkimese were concerned, the right to establish the sanatorium amounted to little more than a temporary lease. However, the British regarded the right as being tantamount to a long lease, with the security of tenure that was normally associated with long lease agreements. These differing views of the word 'right' caused difficult relations between the Sikkimese representative in Darjeeling and the British Superintendent of Darjeeling, Dr Archibald Campbell.

In 1847 Ilam Singh, the Dewan or Chief Minister in Sikkim with whom Campbell had enjoyed cordial relations, died. He was replaced by Tokhang Donyer, a divisive figure of Tibetan descent known in Sikkim as the Pagla Dewan or Mad Dewan. He posted a new representative to Darjeeling with whom Campbell immediately failed to see eye to eye. In 1849, keen to assert his authority, which in Sikkim certainly did not exist, Campbell blundered over the border to meet the king and make representations regarding the suitability of the Sikkim representative in Darjeeling. The Dewan, outraged at Campbell's effrontery, had him arrested before he and the king could meet and he was held for six weeks before release. Campbell was regarded by the British as the architect of his own misfortune caused by his lack of diplomacy. However, despite this blunder, the British felt the need to respond. As Campbell was a British representative, a slight on him was regarded as a slight on the Raj so by way of retribution they annexed 640 square miles of Sikkimese territory adjoining Darjeeling. The machinations and the complexities of the Sikkim court are beyond the scope of this book. Suffice to say these complications led to the arrest by the Sikkim authorities of several ethnic Sikkimese who had sought refuge in the annexed areas. However, the British viewed the arrests as being made on British territory. So in 1860, having been granted permission to carry out a further punitive annexation of another small area of land as further retribution for the 'illegal' arrests, Campbell again marched into Sikkim. However, he marched in with only 100 troops and was promptly ejected. Campbell's reputation was in tatters in the eyes of the Raj and plans were made to replace him. In spite of his ineptness, the British still regarded Campbell as the appointed representative of the Raj and felt that his humiliating ejection from Sikkim was a humiliation for the Raj itself. Therefore, his humiliation needed to be addressed particularly given the damage to British prestige suffered as a result of the 1857 Indian Mutiny. Once more British troops marched into Sikkim, this time on a punitive expedition, but with a stronger force of 2,000 men led by a professional officer, Lieutenant Colonel John Gawler. The expedition was successful and Sikkim, realistically unable to decline British terms, signed the 1861 Treaty of Tumlong which turned the state into a *de facto* British Protectorate. In 1890 Sikkim became what was known as one of the Princely States. It was nominally independent, but under the effective control of the British Raj exercised through a political officer, the Resident, in the capital Gangtok.

In 1879, the first wife of the 9th Maharaja of Sikkim gave birth to a son, Sidkeong Namgyal. Sidkeong was educated firstly at court, then at St Paul's School, Darjeeling prior to attending Pembroke College Oxford. In 1899 he was recognised by the British as heir to the throne of Sikkim, the Maharaj Kumar or Crown Prince of Sikkim.

It had long been a Sikkimese custom that the *Chogyal* or King and Crown Prince would marry a suitable Sikkimese or Tibetan lady, but correspondence from the early 1900s appears to indicate that in the eyes of the palace in Gangtok there existed no such suitable person. Other correspondence from the period, often between Sidkeong and the British Political Resident in Gangtok, demonstrates a strong desire on Sidkeong's part to find a wife. The British were also keen for him to do so, as a marriage would or should guarantee stability in the Kingdom and 'settle' Sikkimese domestic affairs. Therefore, Sidkeong asked the Resident if he would enquire of the Burmese administration whether they could recommend a suitable bride or provide a list of eligible brides from the Burmese aristocracy, a method which would raise eyebrows today; but different times, different mores. The reply from the Government in Rangoon included a list (see page 124) of those deemed to be suitable.

By 1911 Sidkeong's attention was drawn to Princess Ma Lat. A meeting was arranged and subsequent letters between the two suggest that there was a natural attraction over and above the benefit to be derived from the evident social and political suitability. Their courtship, their nascent love affair is touching. Ma Lat's letters to Sidkeong written in the style and the hand of an English public schoolgirl are charming, sometimes naïve, keen, almost desperate to move things on, whilst Sidkeong, also affectionate, seems to be burdened with worry that his father the Maharaja will not sanction his marriage to a non-Tibetan or Sikkimese woman.

Finance was a further cause of concern. The Limbin Prince had only a modest state allowance on which to live and as for Sidkeong, Maharaj Kumar (Crown Prince) or not, Sikkim was not a wealthy country. Sidkeong proposed to Ma Lat who readily accepted his hand in marriage with the proviso that her parents approved of the match. On their consent, Sidkeong Namgyal wrote to the Limbin Mintha and Minthami on 29 July 1913 thanking them for their agreement to the marriage.

The wedding was delayed several times due to the Maharaja's ill health and because it was important to Sidkeong for the court astrologers to approve the proposed dates. Eventually, after many letters and many delays, they settled upon the marriage date of 24 January 1915. However, Sidkeong's father the Maharaja Thutob Mangyal died on 11 February 1914 aged fifty-four. Correspondence sent to Ma Lat by Sidkeong confirm that he had found his father's constant objection to his marriage both difficult to accept, yet equally difficult to ignore. Now the Maharaja's death removed the prime obstacle to his marriage. Sidkeong became *Chogyal* on 10 February 1914 but he did not rule for very long. On 5 December 1914, just six weeks prior to his marriage to Princess Ma Lat, Sidkeong was found dead in the Palace at Gangtok from *'heart failure supervening on an attack of acute jaundice brought on by a severe chill'*.

Sidkeong's death must have come as a devasting blow to Ma Lat and her family. For three years Ma Lat had cultivated a courtship with Sidkeong and looked forward to a life with a man she loved and admired and to a future home together in the Palace on Park Ridge in Gangtok. Her parents, the Limbin Prince and Princess, would have been relieved and happy to see one of their daughters successfully and happily married to a suitable man capable of caring for her. It was unfortunate for Ma Lat, however, that having been engaged to one man, rendered her maritally undesirable to many potentially suitable candidates of a similar lineage and social background. She and her parents would doubtless have quietly despaired of her future. Little exists on record of the family's later life in Rangoon during the dark days of the First World War, but by the war's end Ma Lat was in her mid-twenties and 'on the shelf,' as described by most cultures in the cruel marital terminology of the time.

Life for the Limbin Prince and his family carried on as best it could because there was no other option and Ma Lat had to accept her altered circumstances. In happier days before the war Ma Lat had developed a love of horses and riding. Several of her letters contain references to horses, tack and various other associated equine paraphernalia. Indeed, in a letter to Sidkeong, she mentions that she had on occasion been out riding with the Assistant Commissioner of Police,

Above: Statue of the Prince of Kenaung, brother of King Mindon

Above right: Princess Ma Lat

Right: Sidkeong Namgyal, son of the 9th Maharaja of Sikkim

From: The Political Officer of Sikkim
To: The Maharaj Kumar of Sikkim. 9 October 1910

'I have the honour to enclose a suitable list of ladies in Burma from which you might select a wife and to request that you will kindly let me know whether you desire that further enquiries should be made about any of them.'

List of suitable ladies.

(1) Sao Mya, daughter of the titular Myosa of Indien, and niece of the Swabwa of Yawnghwe. Aged 16. Literate in Burmese.

(2) Sao O, daughter of the Myosa of Mong sit. Aged 17½. Literate in Burmese.

(3) Sao Hawm, daughter of the Laikha Swabwa. Literate (to a moderate extent) in Burmese and Shan. Aged 19.

(4) Sao Hsao, daughter of the Mong Kung Myosa. Aged 17. Illiterate.

These ladies are, as far as can be judged, moral and well brought up, and moderately good looking. Their mothers were commoners, but in Shan opinion the girls take rank from their fathers. No 4 is a particularly attractive and pleasant girl.

The above ladies are daughters of Chiefs of the southern Shan States. They are not of aristocratic lineage on their mothers' side, they have no knowledge of English, and their education in other respects has probably been very slight.

In the Northern Shan States there is one lady, named Nang Sing U, aged 16, the daughter of the Swabwa of south Hsenwi. Her mother is the daughter of the late Htamong of Na-hang Circle, who was a subordinate official. Nang Sing U is literate in Burmese, has no knowledge of English and her educational qualifications are probably about the same as those of the four ladies above mentioned.

Daughters of His Highness the Ex-King of Thebaw :- These ladies are at Ratnagiri.

(1) Teik Su Myat Payagyi   aged 30
(2) Teik Su Myat payalat   "   29
(3) Teik Su Myat paya   "   24
(4) Teik Tin Myat payagale   "   23

It is believed that none of these ladies are acquainted with English.

Daughters of the Limbui Minthn at Allahabad;-

(1) Teik Tin Ma Gyi   aged 20
(2) Teik Tin Ma Lat   "   16
(3) Teik Tin Ma Gale   "   15
(4) Teik Tin Ma Dwe   "   13.

It is believed that all these ladies are acquainted with English. Nos (1) and (3) have passed the Middle School Examination.

THE PRINCESSES

From: Prince Sidkeong Tulku Namgyal
To: Teik Tin Ma Lat
Gangtok
30 May 1913

From: W.H. Hardy, Political Officer
Sikkim Agency Office,
Gangtok
30 June 1913

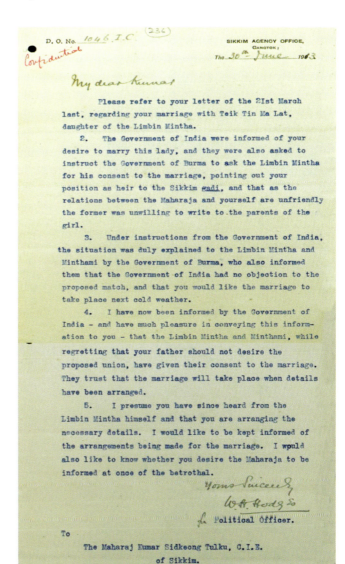

'Yours of the 13 May
Just to hand I am very pleased to hear that the matter reg[arding] our marriage is nearly settled. I have not heard from the Govt. as yet. As regards to the marriage expense the state will grant a sum of money amount as a [con]sequence of my marriage. But I don't think the Maharaja will give me very much because he is dead.'

THE PRINCESSES

From: Prince Sidkeong Tulku Namgyal
To: Prince Limbin Mintha and Mintha Mi
Gangtok
29 July 1913

From Teik Tin Ma Lat
daughter of Prince Limbin Mintha of Burma
To: HH Maharaja Sidkeong Namgyal of Sikkim
2 July 1914

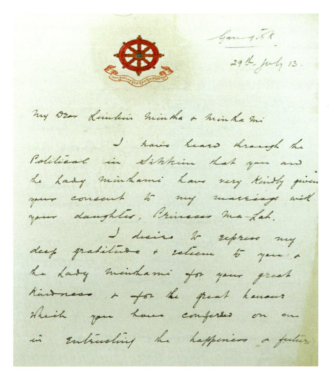

'My Dear Limbin Mintha & Mintha Mi
I have heard through the Political in Sikkim that you and the lady Minthami have very kindly given your consent to my marriage with your daughter, Princess Ma Lat. I desire to express my deep gratitude and esteem to you & the Lady Minthami for your great kindness & for the great honour you have conferred on me in entrusting the happiness and future ...'

Administration Report of the Sikkim State for 1914-1915

Top: Wedding announcement 16 June 1914
Below: Wedding invitation

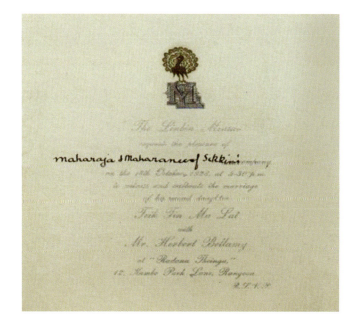

to Sidkeong's very evident displeasure as he made clear in his reply to her. (His notions of proprietary were rooted in Sikkim custom.) Horses and racing in particular were central to social life in Rangoon, the equine epicentres being the Gymkhana Club and the racecourse. Ma Lat often attended race-days at the Rangoon racecourse and whilst placing a bet one day she met by chance an Australian horse-breeder by the name of Herbert Bellamy, who quickly engaged her in conversation offering advice as to likely winners.

Bellamy was very much part of the local Rangoon racing circuit. Until 1911 he had been a partner in Christie & Bellamy, a firm of bookmakers he had co-founded several years earlier and which had taken him to various Straits Settlements, including Bombay, Calcutta and Batavia. Born a first generation Australian to English parents who settled in the State of Victoria in 1878, he was educated locally and went on to study medicine at Melbourne University. However, it seems that medicine quickly bored him; he preferred the life of a swashbuckling character. He tried his luck mining for gold in Kalgoorlie, but lost as much money as he made and he tried sheep farming, but could not stand the smell of the sheep, before finally opening up his firm of bookmakers. Still somewhat unsettled, he took the advice of the Sultan of Johor, a friend and another man with an eye for horses, to go to Burma. This he duly did, settling beside the Rangoon racecourse.

Bellamy and Ma Lat began a liaison, an unlikely courtship for its time and one which was to last several years until Bellamy asked the Limbin Prince for his daughter's hand in marriage. Although he was no Sikkim Prince, Bellamy

Rangoon Racecourse, where Ma Lat first met Australian horse-breeder Herbert Bellamy

was a reasonably successful and popular man with a good reputation. By the time of Bellamy's proposal Ma Lat was thirty-four years old. In those days and at her age she might have been regarded as being firmly on the shelf. However, Herbert Bellamy and Princess Ma Lat were married in 1928 by Indian Civil Service officer Maurice Collis, one of whose many jobs was to act as the Registrar of Births, Deaths & Marriages in Rangoon. In his book *Trials in Burma* Collis describes his impressions of Ma Lat at their first meeting: *'one morning towards the end of 1928 I was sitting in my study when a car drove up to the door and a Burmese woman got out. I went into the hall to receive her. "I am Ma Lat" she said in English, a perfect English without a trace of accent.'* Seated together in his drawing room she told him that she wished him to conduct her wedding ceremony. He noted: *'a beautiful woman in a blue silk skirt and a jacket of white lawn, her complexion corn-coloured, her eyes large and brilliant and with exquisite hands'*. The wedding took place at the Prince's house on 19 October 1928 at precisely 4.48pm. This was the time selected by the astrologers as the most auspicious and as Ma Lat entered the room a clearly smitten Collis saw her wearing: *'a royal* htamein *of oyster coloured silk set with silver diamanté; her hair, in the loose tail style was charged with orchids and there were pearls winding on her throat and breast'*. Herbert Bellamy and Princess Ma Lat were blessed with one child, born on 1 June 1932 and named Princess Yadana Nat Mai, the Goddess of the Nine Jewels – June Rose Bellamy.

Brought up as a Buddhist, yet able to celebrate Christmas and Easter courtesy of her Christian father, June's idyllic childhood was spent in Rangoon happily passing the time between the two different cultures of her parents. She spoke Burmese, Court Burmese, Hindi and English, she helped prepare food for the monks in the mornings and yet could still enjoy Easter eggs in April. Bellamy read the poems of Henry Lawson to Nat Mai and taught her to shoot and ride; he owned and raced a few horses making the occasional book at the Rangoon races. Nat Mai was nine years old when the Japanese bombed Rangoon in February 1942.

So, the family was evacuated to northern India settling again in Allahabad where one of Ma Lat's aunts, who was married to an Indian maharaja, also lived.

June attended St Joseph's Convent School in Kalimpong, Darjeeling, a hill station at around 4,100 feet, whose cool clean air was deemed healthy enough for the British to have opened over a dozen such schools. Her time at the school was memorable only for the difficulties which the nuns seemed to do little to ameliorate. When asked one day if anything was missing from the map of Australia which the nun had displayed, June, remembering a nonsense story read to her by her father put a spot on the centre of the map and said: *'Baragarawindy! A dream country, a land of opposites where the rivers flow inland not out, the leaves grow upwards instead of down, the snakes have feathers and the crows fly*

June and her mother Ma Lat

THE PRINCESSES

June and her father Herbert Bellamy

backwards to keep the dust out of their eyes'. The nun could not or would not relate to such humour, a humour which to modern eyes appears charming and quite poetic. Needless to say, June did not last long at the school.

June was fourteen years old when the family came back to Burma. Rather than return to the Limbin House in Rangoon, they preferred to move back to the Shan hills and Maymyo, where the family originated and where Ma Lat felt at home. Herbert Bellamy was certainly in his element in Maymyo, with a club, a racecourse and easy access to the hills where he could indulge in his new found love of orchid collecting, a hobby at which he became highly proficient and in which he gained a reputation as something of an expert. One cannot help but feel that he and Charlotte Wheeler Cuffe would have enjoyed one another's company.

The travel writer Norman Lewis went to Burma in 1951 and stayed at Maymyo for several days on his way up to Lashio. Maymyo had been bombed by the Japanese during the war and much of the bomb damage still remained. The money spent by soldiers, policemen, Bombay Burmah men and the 'civils' pre-war, had on independence, dried up. Six years on from the end of the war, whilst still retaining some 'magic', the town had become a little down at heel relative to its glory days of the 1920s and 1930s. In his book *Golden Earth*, Lewis appeared to be cautious, restrained, seemingly inconclusive in his observations, almost as if he could not make up his mind about the place. He considered Maymyo to be: *'austere, sporting and contemplative. Maymyo was very clean, hard-working, hard playing, exaggeratedly national and slightly dull. But if unadventurous and simple by French colonial standards* (he was drawing comparisons with French Indochina which he had recently visited), *life in Maymyo was full of solid comfort.'*

It was at dinner with the British Consul, that Lewis met the three Bellamys. He thought Herbert to be: *'genial and confidential'*, Princess Ma Lat he thought looked much less than her fifty-seven years and that: *'her still handsome features*

June in her teens

THE PRINCESSES

Rear row left to right: Princess Ma Lat, three unknown guests, Herbert Bellamy.
Seated: Mario Postiglione, June (Princess Yadana Nat Mai)

Left to right: Herbert Bellamy, Princess Ma Lat (holding Michele) June and Mario Postiglione

were continually enlivened by an expression which made one feel she was amused by something of which she did not entirely approve'. And of June, he thought she had *'allied to the graceful beauty of the Burmese a quite European vivacity'*. He goes on to tell how she was quite able and prepared to 'hot wire' her father's car when it would not start as they prepared to leave.

June was a very bright pupil winning an essay competition sponsored by *The Herald Tribune*. The subject was 'The World We Want', the prize for which was a three-month trip to the USA. She relished the idea of visiting America and she enjoyed the trip tremendously; evidently she was a social 'hit'. While there she made some Hollywood contacts who, as we shall see, came knocking on her door a few years later. She returned to Maymyo to live with her parents, dividing her time between the Shan hills and Rangoon. It was during this period in the capital that she met her first husband.

In the 1950s malaria was still prevalent in many parts of Southeast Asia and the World Health Organisation (WHO) had expert staff working and advising in the capitals of many of the afflicted countries. In Burma, the WHO adviser was an Italian by the name of Mario Postiglione, a bright, well thought of young doctor from Naples and an expert on malaria prevention. June met him in Rangoon in 1953 at one of the many social events to which she was almost automatically invited and embarked, immediately, on a passionate romance, becoming engaged to him within weeks. It was at this point when Hollywood came to see her. She was offered the part of Anna, a young Burmese nurse playing opposite Gregory Peck in the screen adaptation of H.E. Bates' *'The Purple Plain'*. Initially she eagerly accepted but soon withdrew from filming in Ceylon, angered at what she regarded as Hollywood's patronising portrayal of both her native Burma and the Buddhist religion. Her decision took real courage and demonstrated an admirable adherence to principles, given the obvious pecuniary and career benefits which went hand-in-hand with such a screen role: rare courage. She married Mario soon after she returned.

Mario's offices and laboratory had originally been established in Lashio in the Shan hills, but finding the town and the set-up not to his liking, Mario and June moved to Maymyo where their first son Michele was born in May 1955. Seven months later in December, a shocking event took place. Mario was kidnapped at his office in Maymyo by Burmese communists, emboldened perhaps by the visit of Nikita Khruschev to what was an increasingly left-wing country. But the Burmese government refused to negotiate with the terrorists, so it fell to June to handle the negotiations alone, which took courage and inner calm which her Buddhist faith had bestowed upon her. The ransom demand was paid by the WHO and Mario was eventually released unharmed, but traumatised by the shock of the kidnap and his time in captivity. The United Nations instructed the family to leave Burma immediately and they flew out in January 1956. Ten years of WHO postings followed in Geneva, Damascus and later Manila, from where June flew back to Burma to be with her father Herbert when he died in Maymyo. June's second child Maurice was born in 1956 and both boys were sent to Italy to be educated. However, by 1964 the marriage was on the rocks; June and Mario divorced later that year and June moved to Florence settling in the San Frediano district of the city to be close to her sons while they were at school.

In Burma, General Ne Win, a member of the Burmese Independence Army during the Japanese occupation and later second in command to General Smith Dun, had been Prime Minister and Minister for Defence since 1958. In 1962 he formed the Burma Socialist Program Party for which he was both Chairman and President. From these political and military bases he launched his now infamous coup on 2 March 1962 at precisely 2am. Army units seized the Secretariat and other Government sites and arrested President Mahn Win Maung and Prime Minister U Nu and several leading Shan *sawbwas*. At 8:25am, over the Burma Broadcasting Service, armed forces chief General Ne Win announced that the army had taken over government: *'to put a stop to the extremely grave situation that has befallen the Union.'* Later in the morning he set up the Revolutionary Council with himself as Chairman. Almost immediately he issued decrees by which he nationalised private enterprise, hospitals and mission schools, abolished civil and political rights and banned foreign investments and tourism.

This action proved to be disastrous for Burma. *Per capita* income, which had been three times that of Indonesia and twice that of Thailand, fell rapidly until within just a few years Burma had fallen behind both. An impoverished and ruthlessly controlled Burma found itself effectively closed off to the outside world for the next quarter century.

June Bellamy had been mildly acquainted with Ne Win in post-war days when he was a young captain in the Burma Rifles and she knew his wife Khin May Than well. When June's mother Ma Lat became ill in 1965 June applied to the Burmese Embassy in Rome for a visa to return home, but

General Ne Win

The coup on 2 March 1962 at precisely 2am

neither visa nor any form of assistance were forthcoming. She was faced with a rigid bureaucracy which she could not penetrate. In despair she telegrammed Ne Win: *'Mummy's condition critical. Rome embassy incapable of giving me a visa. Please help.'* He did. At once, the embassy called June to say they would meet her at the airport with a visa, but just prior to her flight she received a telegram with news of her mother's death. June did not fly back to Burma, but nevertheless wrote to Ne Win to thank him for his help. Khin May Than, known by many as Katy died in 1972. A year later, Ne Win arranged to meet June whilst on a business trip to Europe. In Burma Ne Win had become very unpopular; his nationalisations and socialist programme had caused economic disaster. Living standards were low, unemployment rife and anti-government demonstrations and riots were becoming more and more frequent. Ne Win made the cold calculation that marriage to June with her aristocratic background might strengthen his support amongst the people. He told June that: *'We* [Burma] *are going towards change. Burma needs you and the people love you.'* Then he proposed. Feeling that as First Lady she could genuinely assist her country June accepted his proposal, *'The family name is still very important in Burma, the royalty, the Limbin',* she later explained and they married in 1976.

After foreign trips with Ne Win to China and Nepal, June realised that there was little she could do to soften her hard and intransigent husband nor to encourage him to change the direction in which he had taken Burma. So after a mere five months and a terrible argument during which he threw an ashtray at her, she left him and her country. Almost as an allegory of Ne Win's failing Burma, the aircraft in which she flew was the only Burma Airways passenger plane to hold international certification of airworthiness for international routes. Shortly thereafter the couple divorced.

Years later in an interview with Desmond O'Grady and Hamish McDonald of *The Griffith Review,* June described her belief that she could have done something for Burma by marrying Ne Win as: *'A sin of pride'; 'I left Burma with*

Princess Yadana Nat Mai, the Goddess of the Nine Jewels – June Rose Bellamy

a definite feeling of failure because I had failed my people. Because they did put their trust in me when I arrived. And this was one of the things that was not liked. But I would rather left as a failure than to be connected with the ruling people. Those who had trusted in me, those who believed in me can say she left, but she left rather than not be able to do anything. In Italian, they say un peccato di orgoglio; in English, a sin of pride. Because I thought I could do something which others had not done. And that's a very bad sin.' Perhaps an overly critical self-assessment of her genuine and well-intentioned efforts.

June returned to Italy in need of income, as neither marriage had 'settled' for her sufficiently. So she decided to set up a cookery school and went to London to train under Kenneth Lo. On returning to Florence in 1983, she established the Associazione Culturale Arte e Gastronomia Orientale to offer cookery classes in Italian and Asian (emphasising Burmese) cuisine. She endured the tragic loss of her youngest son in a car accident in 1991 and sought solace in her family and in hard work. Her business prospered and in 2017 she put her accumulated culinary knowledge down on paper writing *The Soul of Spice*. The book was an almost instant success featuring prominently at the Turin Book Fair.

On 1 December 2020, June Bellamy, Princess Yadana Nat Mai, the Goddess of the Nine Jewels, died suddenly but quietly, during a telephone conversation with a friend. As noted by her son Michele, she had become increasingly *'uncomfortable in this strange world'*: she really did come from somewhere else – another time and place the nature of which is beyond the understanding of most of us. Driven by his interest in his Limbin family Michele had begged her for years to write her autobiography. She relented only towards the end agreeing to permit Italian journalist Francesco Moscatelli to write of her life which was recently published in Italy as *Le Mie Nove Vite* (My Nine Lives).

Press announcement: the wedding of June Bellamy and General Ne Win, 1976

*'Apparently, he had never learned
the gentle art of making enemies
which some find so easy to acquire.'*

Lord Chesterfield

The Artist

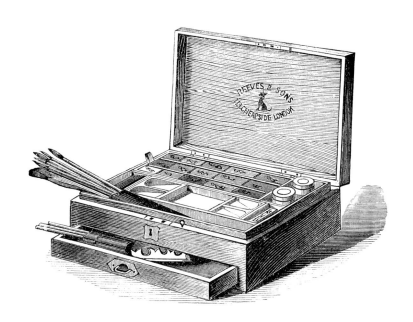

THE ARTIST

Rodway Swinhoe

THE ARTIST

He was a gentle gentleman it would seem; scarce then and even scarcer now. Rodway Swinhoe is the 'Artist' amongst our group of Burmaphiles. He was a gifted and passionate artist, but an amateur through and through. Swinhoe was a successful solicitor who found time to paint, to write and to become deeply and constructively involved in civil society. During his time in Burma he came to be regarded as nothing less than an influential member of the professional and social infrastructure of the country.

When you've seen the great Pagoda and the plains of far Pegu,
And watched the traders trekking to the town of Talifu
You'll be cancelling your ticket – Burma's good enough for you.

So wrote Swinhoe in *'Burma – The Golden Land'*, one of his collection of forty-five poems entitled *Rhymes from Roundabout*, published by the Rangoon Press in 1925. The poem was written during his Burma years. In fact, Swinhoe did 'cancel his ticket' and remained in Burma for thirty-nine years until an early death took him away from his beloved Maymyo at the age of sixty-four.

In his fulsome obituary to Rodway Swinhoe in 1927 Lord Chesterfield, writing in *The Upper Burma Gazette*, described him as a man of many parts; a most accurate description of this multi-talented and capable man. In a tone of restrained melancholy full of praise for Swinhoe, listing his many and various interests and achievements and clarifying just who and what had been lost, Chesterfield pays him this most telling compliment: *'Apparently, he had never learned the gentle art of making enemies which some find so easy to acquire'*.

Rodway Swinhoe was born in Cheltenham in 1863 into a Northumberland family with strong historical links to India. It was a place where many family members had carved out their careers. The first Henry Swinhoe arrived in 1779, followed by three further generations who lived and worked in Calcutta. To this day, several members of the family along with their wives and children, lie underground in Calcutta's Park Street cemetery. In short, most of the Swinhoe family made the Far East their home.

Rodway's great-uncle Robert Swinhoe was born in Calcutta in 1836, then moved to Hong Kong at the age of eighteen with his job at the Foreign Office, having completed his schooling in England. He spent twenty-one years living on the south China coast and on the island of Formosa, where he studied and recorded the birds and butterflies of the island. He worked in such a professional and comprehensive manner that he is regarded as the first naturalist to work on the island. He discovered several new species, two of which, a butterfly and a pheasant, were named after him. At various times he was British Consul to Amoy, Ning-po and Formosa and left the Far East only after a (probable) stroke in 1873. He died four years later at the age of only forty-one; a life full of action, a characteristic not unusual for members of the Swinhoe family during the 1800s.

Rodway studied law and was admitted as a solicitor of the Supreme Court of Judicature in England in 1887. Following the path taken by several other members of his family, he sailed to Calcutta to begin a legal career in India with the family firm Watkins & Swinhoe. However, upon arrival, it became apparent that there was insufficient legal work in Calcutta to keep his bright young mind occupied.

The number of Europeans who normally would have formed a substantial part of his clientele had reduced in part due to the Sepoy Rebellion in 1857. Having sought advice, Swinhoe considered his options and decided to travel further east to Burma, where business was on the increase and the European populace in Rangoon and Mandalay was growing. He sailed to Rangoon in 1888 and in June of that year was admitted to the Court of Judicial Commission in Lower Burma. A short time later he travelled to Mandalay and set up as the first British solicitor to establish a legal presence in Upper Burma. This was a pioneering step and whilst legal work was to be his prime interest, it was not to be his sole business and professional interest for the next thirty years.

Swinhoe's legal activities comprised the whole gamut from criminal damage, illegal liquor sales, marital disputes, labour disputes and on down to the siting and beneficial ownership of wells. His many and various clients were Burman, British, Shan, Karen, Kachin and Indian; it was the stuff of a busy and successful provincial solicitor, a legal pioneer in far flung Mandalay. However, it was his involvement in the second of the ultra-sensitive Ghadar trials for which Swinhoe was selected to sit as one of the Special Tribunal judges, which probably marked the high point of his legal career. The Ghadar movement was primarily a Punjabi revolutionary movement, the aim of which was to expel the British from India. Founded by expatriate Punjabis living in America and Canada, the movement spread back to India, Burma and Singapore. Mutiny was a key part of the movement's plan, but most of the few regiments which were infiltrated had already been penetrated by Police Intelligence. That meant that the mutinies came to little, except for a mutiny by the 5th Light Infantry in Singapore in February 1915. The subsequent Court of Enquiry decided that the poor leadership of the commanding officer and Ghadar-inspired revolutionary fervour were equally to blame for the mutiny. The drive and energy behind the movement petered out and calm was restored following large-scale arrests, a number of lengthy jail sentences and several executions. However, it was a worrying time for the British. The Singapore mutiny and the resultant deaths of over thirty soldiers and civilians focused the collective mind of the Raj. The sensitive, fair, open and even-handed conduct of the Ghadar trial was seen as crucial to future stability in Burma. After the trial, the consensus of opinion was that Swinhoe and other members of the tribunal had performed their roles admirably. But it would be reasonable to assume that the Ghadar leadership might well have taken an entirely different view.

In 1925 aged sixty-two, Swinhoe was admitted as Advocate for the High Court of Judicature in Rangoon and recognised in legal circles as a Judicial Commissioner, in effect a Judge, a position he would have relished. He was known as the Father of the Mandalay Bar. Two years later, upon his death, the occasion was marked by the legal profession when all nine judges of the High Court gathered together in Number 1 Court in Rangoon. They paid tribute to him as the Father, not only of the Mandalay Bar, but of the entire Burma Bar as *The Rangoon Gazette* pointed out; quite a compliment coming from a profession not ordinarily given to hyperbole.

Right from the start Swinhoe appears to have had a strong sense of what was 'fair' and what was not. Furthermore, he possessed a strong sense of civic duty. These virtues were not unusual traits in their time and both manifested themselves in his involvement in the world of 'microfinance'. In 1912 India passed the Cooperative Societies Act; it provided for the establishment of lending institutions which were usually owned by the customers, both depositors and borrowers, of the bank. They would lend money to the self-employed

THE ARTIST

SWINHOE PHEASANTS.
(Eupolocomus swinhoii)

CHOCOLATE TIGER.
(Parantica melaneus)

Above: Robert Swinhoe, aged 27 in 1863

*Above right: Swinhoe Pheasants
(Eupolocomus swinhoii)*

*Right: Chocolate Tiger Butterfly
(Parantica melaneus)*

*Left: Fork-tailed Sunbird
(Aethopyga christinae)*

143

and small businesses, often at generous rates, circumstances where larger commercial banks would not normally become involved. These Cooperative Banks provided a social service for the commercial sector hitherto absent from India and Burma. They were similar in role and outlook to some of the emerging market microfinance institutions of today, which fulfil a much-needed social role. The first such bank to open in Upper Burma was the Upper Burma Central Cooperative Urban Bank Limited and Swinhoe, already renowned for his civic and welfare work, became one of the bank's first Directors. Thus, he became closely involved in the business of fostering the growth of small businesses in Mandalay; crucial work if a local economy is to work effectively.

Swinhoe seldom took long leave in England, but in 1889 he decided to return, not having seen family and friends for years. On this trip Rodway called in to see the Watkins family in Watford – friends who had been one half of an earlier legal partnership in Calcutta. It was at the home of the Watkins family that he met Annie Juxon-Jones and fell in love with her. Annie was the daughter of an East India Company Surgeon Major and was born in Peshawar in northern India. She spent her early years in the country, but like many other children in her position, went back to England for her schooling. She must have shown an aptitude for music, because she spent two years learning the violin at the Brussels Conservatoire and their mutual inclination for

The Upper Burma Central Cooperative Urban Bank Limited

the arts surely must have increased the bond between them. The couple married in Paddington, London, in 1899. After honeymooning in Paris, they returned to England, packed their bags, sailed off to Rangoon, then travelled up-country and set up home in a bungalow on the West Moat Road, Mandalay, to begin their new lives together. Twenty-six years old when she married Swinhoe, Annie produced five children over the following six years. Alas, two of the children did not survive early childhood, but in spite of these setbacks, theirs was a happy and successful marriage. Iris MacFarlane, Annie's granddaughter wrote that they *'remained absorbed in one another and unwearyingly delighted with Burma.'*

Separations were long and painful when the children went back to school in England. Copious accounts exist about the effect on children going back to school at such young ages as well as the effect this had on the parents. But in those days people had to accept this discomfort as part of the price for the pleasure of living in the East. Annie returned to England at three yearly intervals to see the children, but Rodway went back only once in ten years. Part of the reason for these lengthy separations may well have been financial. Rodway was a successful solicitor and a prominent member of the community, but making money was not his forté. He was no spendthrift and nor was Annie, but the indications are that his rainy-day savings were modest and whilst by no means hard up, the Swinhoes were not awash with money. However, they were doing well enough to indulge their love for the Shan hills when they bought a house in Maymyo which they occupied at weekends and holidays over the next twenty years. 'Parkside' was a beautiful colonial hill station bungalow with tall ceilings, wide verandahs and a delightful, well maintained garden which Rodway and Annie enjoyed and often shared with Otway and Charlotte Wheeler Cuffe, with whom the Swinhoes developed a strong friendship. The couple must have spent weeks and months discussing what should be planted in their gardens and consulting with others. The combination of expertise, passion and climate produced delightful results.

Rodway loved orchids. He collected them, he grew them, he became something of an authority on them and sent many specimens to Kew Gardens in London. His love of gardens and his almost permanent addiction to things civic, led to him to become closely involved in the establishment of the Maymyo Botanic Gardens which Charlotte Wheeler Cuffe masterminded, commencing in 1917. (In 1924 the gardens were renamed 'The National Kandawgyi Botanical Gardens'). Rodway Swinhoe's input to the concept and establishment of the gardens and coordination of the project, always the most difficult part, was recognised by naming the Orchid House after him – the Swinhoe Orchid House.

Annie Juxon-Jones, wife of Rodway Swinhoe

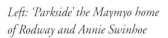

Left: 'Parkside' the Maymyo home of Rodway and Annie Swinhoe

Above: 'Parkside' interior view

Right: Annie and Rodway enjoying their garden at 'Parkside'

In Maymyo, Rodway indulged his other passions, art and writing, which was mainly for the stage. His gift for poetry has been demonstrated through *Rhymes from Roundabout*, but he also loved music and amateur dramatics. In 1909 he wrote *The Cat's Eye*, a Burmese operetta in one act, which was performed in Mandalay later in the same year. He was not so much a performer himself, more a highly energetic composer and in 1910 he teamed up with his friend John Alves, a Captain in the 93rd Burma Infantry. Together they wrote '*Four Songs of Burma*' with words by Swinhoe and music by Alves. They followed this the next year with '*The Golden Land of Burma*' in which, as ever, they talk up their adoptive land:

'Venus Aphrodite was a beauty in her day,
She entered for the Paris stakes and bore the prize away,
But she couldn't hold a candle to a Burma minkalay.'

In 1913 they wrote a musical comedy called *The Palace Plot, or The Maiden Aunt's Revenge*, set in Thibaw's old palace in Mandalay. It was heralded as: 'An entirely new and original Burmese comic opera in two acts,' in which gentle scorn is poured on their 'home' country for its weather and formality:

'There's a gloomy land they tell me
Far beyond the golden West
Where they take their pleasures sadly
And their shopping like the rest
Where you mustn't chaff a damsel
Never bargain for a kiss
But remove your hat politely
And address her just like this –
Fine weather today Miss Brown
Everyone seems to be out of Town
May be just the weekend merely
O! d'you think so? No, not really.
And that's the way you shop in Merry England!

Swinhoe regularly took troupes to play in Rangoon after their initial performances in Mandalay.

His sense of humour and his love for his chosen country is evident in his book, *The Incomplete Guide to Burma*, well illustrated by his friend T. Martin Jones. It is an amusing book, gently teasing, devoid of any colonial pomposity, full of love for Burma and is, if unintentionally so, a 'recruiting' poster for the country.

A little later he wrote *Pictures from Lotus Land*, an affectionate homage to Burma. He loved the country so much that he seems incapable of going any length of time without either writing something about it or painting it. The book was illustrated by his friend F.M. Muriel with the photographs perhaps coming from both.

One of the higher points of Swinhoe's life in Burma and one which was a clear statement of the Government's faith in him was his selection to lead the Burma contingent to the 1924 Empire Exhibition in London.

The object of the exhibition was to demonstrate the bonds and strength of Empire and to show off all things British at a time when the hold on Empire was beginning to weaken despite Britain having only recently emerged victorious from the First World War, or as the event organisers on behalf of the Government put it at the time, they hoped: '*to stimulate trade, strengthen bonds that bind mother Country to her Sister States and Daughters, to bring into closer contact the one with each other, to enable all who owe allegiance to the British flag to meet on common ground and learn to know each other.*' Laudable aims surely and politics aside, the organisers put on a 'good show' and over fifty constituent states of the Empire sent their own representatives to exhibit and show off their country, which indeed they did. The exhibition attracted over twenty-seven million visitors over the course of the eighteen months it was open.

Burma's entry, based around a pavilion and the organisation of the pavilion and its many accoutrements plus the selection of the Burmese team to attend, was a huge task which Rodway took in his stride. Rodway, Annie and the

The entrance to the Burma Pavilion at the British Empire Exhibition, 1924

The Wealth of Burma is displayed in the delightful Burma Pavilion. Skilfully carved ivory figures with specimens of lacquer work, silver and amber are among the exhibits.

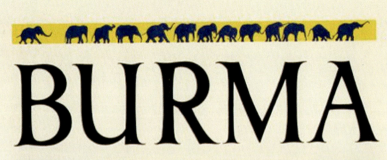

THE ARTIST

Burmese dancers at the British Empire Exhibition, 1924

Burmese team sailed on the *'Amarapoora'* from Rangoon to London in February 1924. The Event Secretary introduced the Burma team thus: 'It was of course and, quite sensibly, very much all about commerce'.

In *Pictures from Lotus Land* we find this piece entitled *'Life in Burma'*. *'Life in Burma is far more simple than it is in the West. The rush and the hurry are absent, because the eager desire for piling up money does not exist. The climate is, for the most part, genial, and daily life flows evenly along, as the broad Irrawaddy slips quietly down to the sea. To the Western visitor, village life in Burma is interesting, but – supremely dull!'*

'No doubt the teachings of Buddhism have something to do with the Burman's outlook on life, but it must be remembered that Buddhism could not have become the national religion unless its teachings had coincided with the character of the people.'

'The Burman can work hard enough when it is necessary to do so, and if he sees no object in putting by for a rainy day, it is because his rainy days are few and far between. Perhaps such a day may never come, and so he spends as he makes, and desires to make no more than he can spend.'

And then there was, of course, Swinhoe's art. He was not a trained artist, he was an enthusiastic, energetic, committed, observant, passionate amateur. All of these virtues are evident in his paintings even to the layman's eye. The harsh critic, more concerned with purist execution, might have a field day. Some faces are unclear, some arms too long and so on. It is easy to find fault if one tries, but Swinhoe was a lawyer, he spent his working hours behind a desk pouring over legal documents. He did not have the luxury of spending the hours he would have liked at his easel. He needed to do his legal work that paid the bills. But this untrained artist could capture the mood of the countryside and convey through his brush a love for Burma. And, with a lawyer's forensic eye, his work forms a record of those who mattered, the people, their clothes and dress at a specific period of time.

In the foreword to her novel *The Lacquer Lady* set in Mandalay, writer, journalist and criminologist Fryniwyd Tennyson Jesse, the great-niece of Alfred Lord Tennyson, gave profuse thanks and gratitude to Rodway Swinhoe for all the help and advice he had given to her in the production of her book. In fact, so comprehensive was his knowledge of Upper Burma and Thibaw's old court and so fulsome were his explanations, that she based the book very largely on what Swinhoe had told her. His contributions were generous and the book became a minor modern classic.

On 4 August 1927 while at work in his office in Mandalay, Swinhoe complained of feeling unwell and went home to West Moat Road. Annie, then in Maymyo, was contacted and went to him immediately. There was no improvement the following day. Later that morning he said that he was feeling very tired, then he rolled over onto his side and quietly died; he was sixty-four years old. He was buried in Christ Church Cemetery, Mandalay, the next day.

The death of Rodway Swinhoe must have been mourned by many. A collection was arranged to raise money for a monument to him in Maymyo. The memorial to Swinhoe was not a simple stone or wall-mounted brass, appreciated as either would have been, but a pair of beautiful stained-glass windows installed in All Saints Church. Quite a testimony. The windows were badly damaged by the Japanese army during the war, but then in the early 2000s, over three quarters of a century after Swinhoe's death, local people again raised money for them to be restored. Memories can last a long time.

Annie, widowed at an early age, was lonely without the man with whom she had spent happy decades in Maymyo and Mandalay and in whom she had been 'absorbed'. Alone, with no means of support, she left Burma, a huge wrench after living in the country for nearly three decades. She spent her remaining years in London in her small, 3rd floor flat in Notting Hill Gate and died in 1956. She never remarried.

Above: Sketch by Rodway Swinhoe of his wife Annie on board the steamer Manora, 1889

Right: Stained-glass windows at All Saints Church, Maymyo, installed in memory of Rodway Swinhoe

Paintings by F.M. Muriel taken from Pictures from Lotus Land *described by Rodway Swinhoe*

THE ARTIST

Paintings of Burma by Rodway Swinhoe

Captain A Defying the Kachins

Captain A Recounting His Adventures

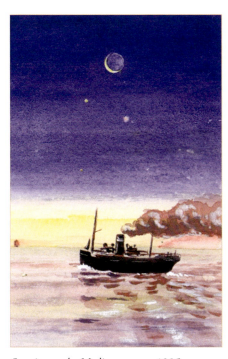

Sunrise on the Mediterranean, 1895

Sketches by Rodway Swinhoe *Riverboat on the Irrawaddy*

People taking tea beside the moat which surrounds the city walls of Mandalay, c1920

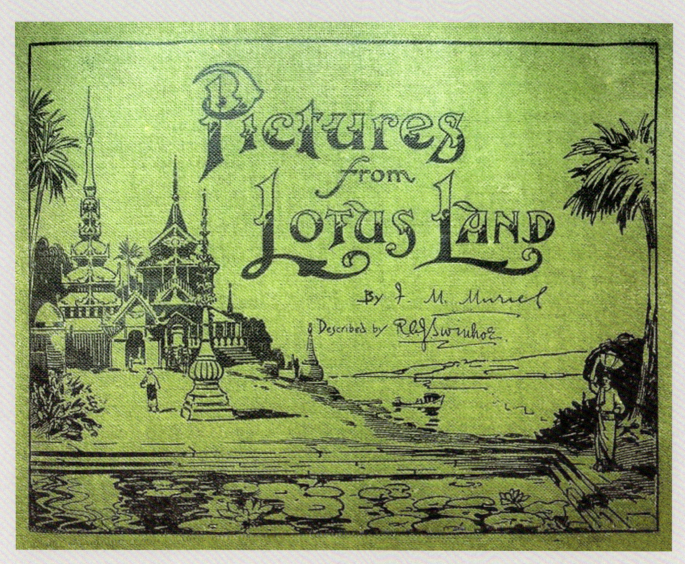

Pictures from Lotus Land
Author: F.M. Muriel
Described by: Rodway Swinhoe
Publisher: Rangoon: Rowe & Company
[1924]

RANGOON.

Yet perhaps it seems a pity
Not to wander through the city
Not to see the Gym and Zoo
And the great Pagoda too.
So, if time will not permit,
Ask the train to wait a bit.

Later, when the moon is out
Take a boat and row about,
Watch the flying fishes play
In some well secluded bay
You can catch them with a spoon
At the Boat Club in Rangoon.

THE MINKALAY.

Never mind what people say
Here's your health, fair Minkalay.
Roses in your raven hair
Silken skirt of pattern rare,
Sandalled feet that peep beneath,
Laughing eyes and pearly teeth;
Though your fashions may disclose
Neither frills or furbelows
Though you know not Worth nor Jay
You're a picture Minkalay.
Mingling with the daily strife
In the heat and dust of life
Toiling on the open trail
Scornful of the purdah's veil,
Smoothing life's uneven way
You're no coward, Minkalay.

Pages from The Incomplete Guide to Burma
Words by Rodway Swinhoe
Illustrated by T. Martin Jones

THE RESOLVE.

If, distressed by social ills,
Taxes, Wars, Insurance Bills,
Tired of home, you seek to view
Greener fields and pastures new;
If, in short, you wish to know
Some convenient place to go.

Do not stop to look about you
Home can get along without you,
Do not wait to wonder how
Take a ticket here and now.
Do not waste one precious day
Book your seat to Mandalay.

Make your Will, insure your life,
Don't forget to kiss your wife
Fling the children from your neck,
Shed a tear and rush on deck.

Sketches of Maymyo people by Rodway Swinhoe

'For over fifty years into the early twentieth century, Beato's photographs of Asia constituted the standard imagery of travel diaries, illustrated newspapers, and other published accounts, and thus helped shape 'Western' notions of several Asian societies.'

L. Gartlan

The Photographer

THE PHOTOGRAPHER

At the turn of the 20th century Mandalay housed a European population figuring in the hundreds. It was likely, therefore, that most people knew one another; one of the pleasures, or curses, of smaller societies. It was whilst in Mandalay that Rodway Swinhoe came to know the Anglo-Italian photographer Felice Beato, considered by many to be the father of modern photojournalism. It is a stretch of the imagination to include Beato amongst the Maymyo people about whom we have chosen to write. As far as we know, he did not reside in Maymyo for any length of time, nor do we have evidence to suggest that he succumbed to the Shan hills' air. But we do know that this widely travelled photographer did succumb to Burma. He settled in Mandalay where he established a photographic studio and an antiques and curios shop and remained there for almost twenty years. Furthermore, we know that he took several photographs in Maymyo depicting Shans, British soldiers and settlers. Therefore, he probably sojourned in Maymyo, as commuting back and forth from Mandalay was not an option in those days. It is apparent that Rodway Swinhoe acquired a number of his photographs that are now in the possession of his family, some of which are reproduced in this chapter of the book.

By the time Beato arrived in Burma in 1886 he was in his mid-fifties and had earned an international reputation as a superb and well-travelled photographer.

Felice Beato

One of four children, Felice Beato was born in Venice in 1832. When he was two years old the family moved to the British Protectorate of Corfu, where they lived for ten years before moving on to Constantinople in 1844. The celebrated Constantinople-based, British photographer James Robertson met, courted and in 1854 married Beato's sister Leonilda Maria Matilda. It was through Robertson that Beato learned the art and science of photography. He became Robertson's photographic assistant and around 1855 joined Robertson on a foray across the Black Sea to take photographs of the Crimean War. Robertson, Beato and others produced some extraordinary photographs of the war, including shots of the Balaklava Valley through which galloped The Light Brigade, immortalised in Alfred Lord Tennyson's poem *'The Charge of the Light Brigade'*.

Beato spent two years in India during the latter stages of the Sepoy Rebellion which began in 1857 and which rumbled on until 1860. He went on to photograph one of the most iconic and frequently reproduced of all his pictures, the Secundra Bagh after it was stormed by the 93rd Highlanders and the 4th Punjab Regiment. He went to China in 1860 during the Second Opium War, during which it appears that he met Robert Swinhoe, then acting as an interpreter

for the British forces. He also encountered Charles Wirgman, a writer for *The Illustrated London News*. In 1863 he moved to Japan where he spent twenty-one years producing some of the country's most historic images during the years of transition through the Shogun and into the Meiji period. There he employed to great effect, the pioneering hand-colouring skills of the brilliantly gifted Wirgman, later to become his business partner.

Beato claimed to have arrived in Burma in 1886 and in the book *Wanderings in Burma*, by G.W. Bird, which contained over thirty of Beato's photographs, the author suggests the same date. However, the first photograph of Burma credited to Felice Beato was taken in December 1889 depicting the grounds of Government House in Mandalay. In 1890 he set up his studio with three photographic assistants, B. Ryan, H. Smith and F. Bareilly. Shortly thereafter, Beato expanded the studio to include a curio shop – presumably filled with trinkets and artefacts he had acquired on his travels. Later on he opened another curio and antiques shop in Phayre Street, Rangoon in 1901.

In 1871 English photographer and physician Richard Leach Maddox invented the gelatin plate method of photography, an easier and faster process by which commercial operatives could develop their plates. Recognising this, Beato seized on the process which enabled him to photograph various sites around Mandalay and Mandalay Palace extensively, much of his work being reproduced in *The Illustrated London News*, in Alice Hart's *Picturesque Burma* and in George Bird's

Long boat. Albumen print. Late 19th century

Wanderings. When Beato accompanied General Sir George Wolsley's punitive expedition to suppress the *Sawbwa's* rebellion in Wuntho, 180 miles north of Mandalay, he discovered that gelatin plates were ideally suited to action photography.

By the turn of the century, the evolving and increasingly competitive photographic environment was making it more difficult for photographers to earn a living. More and more of them were entering the profession, each taking a slice of the market share. Watts & Skeen, a prominent force in the profession was taken over by Beato, but almost immediately, key staff exited the firm and formed Wagstaffe & Company, yet another competitor. P. Klier & Company was cleverly and conveniently placed for the tourist trade, situated right next to Thomas Cook on Signal Pagoda Road. Then when Eastman Kodak produced the Box Brownie camera in 1900, much of Beato's trade disappeared almost overnight. To compound matters, around 1912, Indian photographer and postcard publisher D.A. Ahuja entered the fray and swamped the market with his own photographs and work by others including Beato. However, by this time, around 1906, Beato had left Burma for good. He died in Florence in 1909 in modest financial circumstances, but with his legacy intact. His renown as a founder of modern photojournalism, is one which one can safely assume he would have preferred to the accumulation of great wealth.

Anne Lacoste's wonderful book *Felice Beato: A Photographer on the Eastern Road* is unbeatable for those who wish to read about his life before Burma.

Mandalay Palace moat, east wall and bridge. Albumen print. Late 19th century

Mandalay Palace. Albumen print. Late 19th century

Family of Saopha (ruler), Wuntho. Albumen print. Late 19th century

Girls waiting at the temple. Albumen print. Late 19th century

Burmese lady and her attendants. Albumen print. Late 19th century

IFC paddle steamers on the Irrawaddy River. Albumen print. Late 19th century

Stern of a Burmese barge. Albumen print. Late 19th century

THE PHOTOGRAPHER

Burmese family. Albumen print. Late 19th century

Anara Pagoda. Albumen print. Late 19th century

Nine dacoits with their captors. Albumen print. Late 19th century

Ten dacoits. Albumen print. Late 19th century

Two crucified dacoits. Albumen print. Late 19th century

Fighting in the jungle during the annexation of Wuntho. Albumen print. Late 19th century

Mingun Bell. Once the heaviest functioning bell in the world. Albumen print. Late 19th century

Mandalay race course. Albumen print. Late 19th century

'Misery seemed to have no place in this land of delight, but contentment ever reigns and the happy Burman dreams away his life in a paradise of sunshine.'

Beth Ellis

The Stayers On

THE STAYERS ON

Not all of the British went 'Home', some because they died before they could, others because they simply did not wish to leave the Shan hills. The cemetery by the former Garrison Church in Maymyo is where all of the British who either could not or chose not to return to England were eventually laid to rest. The passage of time has taken its toll on the cemetery, a cemetery which contains around 303 graves of which 200 are those of soldiers, the remainder being either their dependants or civilians. The earliest grave was dug in 1895 and the most recent, 1973.

THE STAYERS ON

Bibliography

Ardeth Maung Thawaghmung. *The Karen Revolution in Burma: Diverse Voices, Uncertain Ends.* East West Centre, Washington, 2008.

Bowden, Ann and Adams, Ian. *Ever Your Loving Mully,* 2008.

Collis, Maurice. *Lords of The Sunset – A Tour in the Shan States.* Faber and Faber, 1938.

Collis, Maurice. *Trials in Burma.* Faber and Faber, 1938.

Croke, Vicki Constantine. *Elephant Company.* Random House, 2014.

Data Paper No 113, May 1980.

Ellis, Beth. *An English Girl's First Impressions of Burmah.* R Platt, Wigan, 1899.

Ellis, Miles. *Elizabeth (Beth) Ellis: A Short History,* (Unpublished essay).

Ellis, Miles. Correspondence with, 2020-2021.

Hunt, Gordon. *The Forgotten Land.* Geoffrey Bles, London, 1967.

Jansen, Berthe. *The Monastic Guidelines by Sidkeong Tulku; Monasteries, Sex and Reform in Sikkim.* Journal of the Royal Asiatic Society, Third Series, Volume 24, No.4, October 2014.

Kinsman, Darren. A. *A Descriptive Analysis of F. Beato & Co's Commercial Souvenir Album,* Photographic Views and Costumes of Japan, held at George Eastman House, 1993.

Kipling, Rudyard. *From Sea to Sea, Letters of Travel 1899-1913.* MacMillan and Company London, 1920.

Lacoste, Anne. *Felice Beato, A Photographer on the Eastern Road.* J. Paul Getty Museum, 2010.

Lewis, Norman. *Golden Earth.* Jonathan Cape, 1952.

London Gazette, Supplements to: 28th October 1942, 5 April 1945 and 17 January 1946.

Macfarlane, Prof. Alan. Conversations and correspondence with and access provided to papers and artwork of his great grandfather, Rodway Swinhoe, plus access to papers and photographs of Felice Beato.

Macfarlane, Iris. *Daughters of the Empire: A Memoir of Life and Times in the British Raj.* OUP India, 2006.

Marsh, David. *An Amateurish Effort? The Foundation of the National Botanic Gardens of Burma,* 1914-1922. Garden History, Vol 43, No2. The Gardens Trust, 2015.

McKay, Alex. *The Anglo-Sikkim War of 1861*, Bulletin of Tibetology. XXXX 1.2, 2016.

Morshead, Ian. *The Life and Murder of Henry Morshead.* The Oleander Press, 1982.

Nelson, E Charles. *Shadow Among Splendours.* National Botanic Gardens, Glasnevin, Ireland, 2013.

Past Forward, Issue No71. Wigan Museums and Archives, December 2015.

Pointon, AC. *The Bombay Burmah Trading Corporation Limited 1863-1963.* The Millbrook Press, 1964.

Postiglione, Michele Bellamy. Conversations with, 2021.

Princess Hope Leezum of Sikkim. Correspondence with, 2021.

Slim, Field Marshal Sir William. *Defeat into Victory*. Cassell & Co. Ltd, 1956.

Smith Dun, General, *Memoirs of the Four Foot Colonel*. Cornell University, Southeast Asia Program.

The Burma Campaign. burma@rothwell.force9.co.uk

Theroux, Paul. *The Great Railway Bazaar*. Hamish Hamilton, 1975.

Thirkell-White, Sir Herbert. *A Civil Servant in Burma*. Edward Arnold, London, 1913.

Sources

Minus, Sharman. Chasing Chinthes Website.

Sikkim Palace Archives, Gangtok, Sikkim.

The National Archives, Kew, London.

The National Army Museum, London.

The Royal Ark Website.

Acknowledgements

Special thanks to Professor Alan Macfarlane and Sarah Harrison for their generous and extensive help regarding the life of their ancestor Rodway Swinhoe, for access to his artwork and papers and for permission to use photographs taken by Felice Beato, held in their private collection.

Unpublished Crown Copyright documents in the Oriental and India Office Collection appear by permission of Her Majesty's Stationery Office.

The author, editor and publisher have made every effort to trace the copyright holders of prints and photographs. If any individuals or institutions are incorrectly credited or if there are any other omissions, we would be glad to be notified so that the necessary corrections can be made in any reprint.

Thanks to those whose images have been included in this book, including; Friern Barnet & District Local History Society, p.62; Dominic Faulder, pp.25, 48, 49; David May, pp.189, 190, 191; Christopher Harrison for providing many of the cemetery photos, pp.188-191

The author is indebted to The Botanic Gardens at Glasnevin in Dublin for their kind provision of photographs of artwork by Charlotte Wheeler Cuffe.

Thanks to Miles Heffernan for his patient collation and organisation of illustrations.

A RARE EARLY PHOTOGRAPH OF CHARLOTTE CUFFE'S BOTANIC GARDEN, c.1920...

... AND HER 'GANG OF LABOURERS'

MAYMYO The Civil Hospital

MAYMYO The Telegraph Office